Celebrating California

*Recipes that turn any meal
into a celebration*

CHILDREN'S
HOME
SOCIETY OF
CALIFORNIA

**Edited by:
Joyce L. Hyde**

Profits from sales of this cookbook benefit children and families by supporting the services of Children's Home Society of California (CHS).

Many of these children have experienced abuse and neglect. At CHS they are given shelter, care, and the treatment services that will enable them to overcome the past and grow into healthy adulthood. Some of these children have parents who love them, but need a helping hand from CHS to get through a crisis. Whatever the situation, CHS is there — protecting children and preserving families, as we have done since 1891.

While you are enjoying your cookbook, remember that our best recipe is one you won't find in these pages. It's the CHS recipe for giving a better life to a child. The vital ingredients are dedicated volunteers, skilled staff, and generous donors — including everyone who has helped by purchasing this cookbook. We thank them all.

Printed in the USA by

WIMMER
The Wimmer Companies, Inc.
Memphis • Dallas

Introduction

Californians, it seems, can always find a reason to celebrate. A holiday, a birthday, a sports event, an important date in history, or the achievement of a personal milestone — these are a few of the reasons that bring family and friends together for special foods and traditions.

Many of our celebrations center around the bounty of the land and the sea. Festivals abound in California, as communities celebrate the foods that have made them famous and prosperous.

Celebrating California, our second collection of recipes from the good cooks of Children's Home Society of California, captures the flavor of these good times. Come share our family celebrations, with dishes that reflect our state's rich ethnic and cultural diversity. Enjoy new ways of presenting California's fresh fruits, vegetables, and seafoods. Travel with us to several of the state's popular food celebrations, as we sprinkle these pages with award-winning recipes from the Garlic, Artichoke, Strawberry and other festivals.

We invite you to use this book to create your own celebrations in the California style, enjoying the abundance of good foods and the spirit of friendliness and hospitality which are so much a part of our Golden State.

Acknowledgements

EMPORIUM

WEINSTOCKS

THE BROADWAY

Celebrating California

Committees

COOKBOOK COORDINATOR
Joyce L. Hyde

STAFF SUPPORT
Sue Bubnack
Caryl Hansen

ADVISORY COMMITTEE
Diane Rogers, *Chair*
Benella Bouldin
Fran Curtis
Lillian Heintz
"Boots" Murphy
Barrie Wentzell

SELECTION COMMITTEE
Fran Curtis
Barrie Wentzell

COMPUTER TYPING AND EDITING
Fran Curtis
Ruth Paz

ARTIST
Trudi Crockett

VERSES
Bee De Prez

HINTS FOR LOWERING THE FAT IN YOUR DIET
Dianne Tibbs

For freely giving of his time and expertise we also wish to thank:
Charles L. Hyde

4

Table of Contents

Hints For Lowering the Fat in Your Diet

Americans are more aware of the impact that nutrition can have on our health today than ever before. We are well aware that the American fat-rich diet leads us to a variety of diseases including; heart disease, stroke, diabetes, some forms of cancer, (breast, prostate, colon), and obesity to name a few.

Despite all of the information and statistics that we read every day urging us to reduce our fat intake, we still consume about 40% of our daily calories from fat. That's equivalent to about eight tablespoons of fat or one stick of butter!

The American Heart Association and The National Cancer Institute recommend that we reduce our fat intake to 30% or less per day. Many health professionals recommend 20% or less a day, particularly for those who wish to lose weight. Of course the most complete health plan includes:

1. A sensible eating plan that is:
   a. high in fiber
   b. low in fat
   c. high in complex carbohydrates

2. Aerobic and strength training exercises

3. Lots of good clean water

Now let's get to those easy solutions and substitutions!

1. Read labels! Many are misleading!!

2. Know how to calculate the percentage of calories from fat. All calories are not created equal. There are 9 calories in one gram of fat. If you want to know the percentage of food that is fat, learn the formula below.
   a. Take the number of fat grams x 9, then divide that number by the total calories. That will give you the percentage of calories that come from fat. For example, one cup of whole milk contains 150 calories and 8 grams of fat.

   $$8 \times 9 = 72 \text{ fat calories}$$
   $$72 \text{ divided by } 150 = 48$$

This means that 48% of the calories in whole milk come from fat! That is almost half of the calories. If you insist on drinking milk, maybe it's time for you to switch to skim milk!

3. Avoid meats high in saturated fat, such as bacon, sausage and luncheon meats (try to avoid nitrites). Eat more turkey, chicken and fish.

4. If you eat red meat, trim off all visible fat. A 4-ounce T-bone steak broiled has 27.9 fat grams (untrimmed).

5. Choose white meat chicken or turkey and always skin before cooking. Example, a 4-ounce serving of roasted chicken breast without skin has 3.1 fat grams. A 4-ounce serving of roasted chicken breast with skin has 7.6 fat grams. Chicken is a good choice on a low fat diet, but if prepared the wrong way, the value can be easily offset. Example, a 4-ounce serving of half chicken breast prepared at a fast food restaurant can contain up to 24.0 fat grams per serving!

6. Substitute egg whites or egg substitutes for whole eggs.

7. Avoid high cholesterol foods, such as liver and other organ meats.

8. Avoid whole milk and whole milk products. Use 1% or 2% low fat or non-fat milk products, i.e., cheese, cottage cheese, yogurt, etc.

9. Sauté in wine, fat-free chicken and beef broth, spices, flavored vinegars and juices from fresh vegetables. Use non-fat cooking spray.

10. If you must use oil - choose wisely. Use olive oil or canola oil that is lower in saturated fat. A recipe rarely needs as much oil as called for, so decrease the amount needed.

11. For thickening sauces, substitute pureed vegetables for cream or whole milk.

12. Use powdered low-fat or skim milk instead of non-dairy creamer.

13. Replace baking chocolate with cocoa powder. Three tablespoons cocoa powder equal one square chocolate.

14. Cook in a nonstick pan using a small amount of oil or cooking spray.

15. Replace ⅓ to ½ the amount of fat in your recipe with equal amounts of water or juice.

16. Always be alert for and use low-fat and non-fat foods whenever possible.

Healthy Substitutions

RECIPE CALLS FOR:	USE:
Butter or margarine	Fat-free margarine
Chocolate	Fat-free fudge topping or cocoa
Cream cheese	Fat-free cream cheese
Cream	Evaporated milk
Ice cream	Frozen non-fat yogurt or non-fat ice cream
Margarine or oil for baking	Applesauce or prune paste. (Use equal amounts)
Luncheon meats	Water packed tuna or low-fat turkey slices
Salad dressings	Fat-free dressings
Hamburger	Ground turkey
Mayonnaise	Fat-free mayonnaise
Pasta	Any kind except those with egg yolks
Cake	Angel food cake, low-fat cake mixes or homemade with fat modifications

We are in the midst of a "Fat Revolution" in this country and food companies are just starting to respond positively to the high demand for non-fat and low-fat product lines. Many new products are coming to your supermarket shelves weekly. Don't be afraid to experiment and find the brand that you like the best! *Bon Appetit!*

> *The battle of cholesterol*
> *Provides an ongoing test for all;*
> *The searchers' goal in this*
> *quest for all*
> *Is a single answer that's best for all.*

Appetizers
&
Beverages

California Avocado Festival
Carpinteria, CA

CALIFORNIA AVOCADO FESTIVAL
P. O. Box 146
Carpinteria, CA 93013
(805) 684-0038

The annual *California Avocado Festival* honors the popular green fruit with avo-tivities galore, the first weekend in October. The avocado will be showcased in a tasty array of international food booths. Other festival features include global music, The Magic Moonshine Theater, a huge arts and crafts fair, The Carpinteria Flower Show, a farmers' market, the "Little Dip" Triathlon, the "Big Avocado" four-mile run and much more.

Stockton Asparagus

FESTIVAL VIII

STOCKTON ASPARAGUS FESTIVAL
1132 North Hunter Street
Stockton, CA 95202
(209) 466-6653

The *Stockton Asparagus Festival* heralds the spring asparagus harvest with the mouthwatering aromas and flavors of asparagus as prepared fresh on site by volunteers. Other highlights are the Concours d'Elegence, arts and crafts, live entertainment, fun run, and horse and wagon rides.

Ceviche

1. Cut seafood into small pieces. Marinate fish in lime juice overnight.

2. Gently toss avocado, scallions, tomatoes, cilantro and green chiles with fish mixture.

3. Combine oil, wine and oregano. Pour oil mixture over fish and gently toss again. Chill until served. Yield: 4 servings.

"The Avocado Lovers' Cookbook", Joyce Carlisle; copyright 1985, Celestial Arts.

½ **pound seafood (halibut, sea bass, salmon, snapper, lobster, crab, or scallops)**
½ **cup lime juice**
1 **avocado, diced**
2 **tablespoons scallions, chopped**
1 **medium tomato, seeded and chopped**
3 **tablespoons fresh cilantro leaves (1 tablespoon dried, crumbled)**
2 **tablespoons diced green chiles**
1 **tablespoon salad oil**
1 **tablespoon red wine**
1 **tablespoon fresh oregano, chopped (1 teaspoon dried, crumbled)**

A tempting and tasty hors d'oeuvre
Is our favorite morsel to serve;
If we show and tell it,
Don't ask us to spell it;
Most of us don't have the nerve.

PRIZE WINNER • STOCKTON ASPARAGUS FESTIVAL

Asparagus and Mussels Vinaigrette

½ **cup olive oil**
3 **tablespoons red wine vinegar**
2 **teaspoons capers**
1 **small onion, minced**
1 **tablespoon minced red peppers (pimento)**
1 **tablespoon minced parsley**
  salt and pepper to taste
1½ **pounds fresh asparagus**
2 **pounds medium mussels**
1 **slice lemon**
1 **cup water**

1. Prepare 1 day in advance.

2. In a bowl whisk the oil and vinegar, then add the capers, onion, red peppers, parsley, salt and pepper. Set aside.

3. Cut the asparagus into ¼ inch slices (diced), then blanch in boiling water for 3 minutes. Let cool.

4. Scrub the mussels well, removing the beards. Discard any that do not close tightly. Place 1 cup water in a skillet with the lemon slice. Add the mussels and bring to a boil. Remove the mussels as they open. Cool. Remove the mussel meat from the shells and mix it into the vinaigrette with the asparagus. Cover and refrigerate overnight.

5. Reserve ½ the mussel shells, clean them well, and place them in a plastic bag in the refrigerator. Before serving, place the mussel-asparagus mixture in the shells and spoon a small amount of the vinaigrette over each one.

Tomas Lucia

Herbed Shrimp Spread

1. Drain and mash shrimp. Mix together with remaining ingredients. Refrigerate at least 3 hours, preferably overnight. Serve on crackers or flat bread. Yield: 8 to 10 servings.

1   (4½ ounce) can small shrimp
1   (8 ounce) package cream cheese
3   tablespoons mayonnaise
½   lemon, juice only
¼   teaspoon dill weed
3   green onions, minced
2   chicken bouillon cubes

Perfect Shrimp Dip

1. Lightly combine all ingredients. Refrigerate for at least 6 hours before serving. Serve with vegetable thins or garlic rounds. Yield: 8 to 10 servings.

2   carrots, grated
1   bunch radishes, grated
1   bunch onions (tops included), chopped
⅔   cup small cooked shrimp
½   teaspoon Worcestershire sauce
½   teaspoon garlic salt
¼   teaspoon pepper
2   cups mayonnaise

Caviar Pie

1. Mix eggs and mayonnaise. Line bottom of 8 inch pie pan with mixture. Layer onions on top. Mix cream cheese with sour cream. Layer over onions. Chill mixture 3 hours or overnight. Top with caviar and serve. Yield: 8 to 10 servings.

6   hard cooked eggs, chopped
3   tablespoons mayonnaise
½   cup green onion, chopped
1   cup yellow onion, chopped
1   (8 ounce) package cream cheese
⅔   cup sour cream
3½ ounces lumpfish caviar

Solana Shrimp Salsa

1½ cups fresh or frozen white corn
1 (15 ounce) can black beans, rinsed
1 medium zucchini, julienne sliced
1 avocado, diced
¾ cup red onion, diced
1¼ pounds large shrimp, peeled, deveined, cooked and sliced lengthwise

Dressing:
3 small green onions, diced
¾ cup fresh cilantro, (leaves only)
¾ cup fresh lime juice
1 tablespoon vegetable oil
1 small jalapeño or serrano chile, halved and seeded
   salt to taste

1. Mix dressing in blender. Toss with other ingredients. Can marinate for 24 hours. Serve with corn chips.

Can be served over red leaf lettuce as a salad.

Be very careful handling the chile, it can burn.

Stuffed Clams

1 large clove garlic, finely minced
1 tablespoon diced onion
1 teaspoon fresh parsley, finely chopped
2 tablespoons olive oil
¼ cup bread crumbs
¼-½ teaspoon oregano
1 (6½ ounce) can minced clams, not drained
   salt to taste
   Parmesan cheese

1. Sauté the garlic and onion in the olive oil. Add parsley, bread crumbs, oregano, stir. Add clams, clam juice and salt. Spoon mixture into clam shells and dust with a little more bread crumbs and sprinkle Parmesan cheese on top. Bake at 375 degrees for 20 to 30 minutes or until bubbly and crusty. Serve with forks. Yield: 4 to 6 servings.

Corn Dip

1. Mix sour cream, mayonnaise, and salt. Add corn, green pepper, green onions. Mix. Add cheddar cheese. Serve with assorted crackers. Yield: 8 to 12 servings.

½ cup mayonnaise
½ cup sour cream
¼ teaspoon salt
1 (12 ounce) can corn, drained
½ green pepper, chopped
2 green onions, chopped
¾ pound sharp cheddar cheese, shredded

Caponata Dip

1. Heat olive oil in a very large skillet. Sauté the eggplant for about five minutes, until soft. Add remaining ingredients, except the pita bread. Cook over medium heat for about 25 minutes or until most of the liquid evaporates. Serve with pita triangles for dipping. Yield: 12 to 16 servings.

Chopped black or green olives may be added or substituted for the capers.

⅔ cup olive oil
1 large eggplant (do not peel), cut into ½ inch cubes
1 zucchini, diced
4 cloves garlic, crushed
1 onion, chopped
2 tablespoons capers
2 (14½ ounce) cans Italian style tomatoes, chopped and slightly drained
1 tablespoon red wine vinegar
1 teaspoon sugar
½ teaspoon Italian herbs dash of salt and pepper pita bread, cut into triangles

Holiday Dip

1 cup mayonnaise
1 (8 ounce) container
sour cream
1 (8 ounce) can water
chestnuts, drained and
chopped
2 tablespoons chopped
pimento
1 tablespoon sliced
green onion
2 teaspoons beef
flavored granular
bouillon
½ teaspoon
Worcestershire sauce
¼ teaspoon garlic powder
fresh vegetables or
potato chips

1. Combine all ingredients except
vegetables or chips. Mix well. Cover
and chill. Stir before serving. Serve
with vegetables or chips for dipping.
Yield: 10 to 12 servings.

Peanut Fruit Dip

1 (8 ounce) package
cream cheese,
softened
¾ cup brown sugar
1 teaspoon vanilla
1 cup salted peanuts,
chopped

1. Mix all ingredients in a food processor. Serve as dip for sliced fruit.

Artichoke Pâté

1. Cut cheese into 1 inch cubes and place in food processor. Chop. Add remaining ingredients and process for 1 minute. If too thick, add some of the reserved marinade. Place in mold or crock and chill. Serve with crackers. Will keep several days in refrigerator, or can be frozen for several months. Yield: 2 cups.

½ teaspoon grated onion
1 (6 ounce) jar marinated artichoke hearts, drained (reserving marinade)
½ teaspoon Worcestershire sauce
½ teaspoon oregano
1-2 tablespoons fresh lemon juice
1 (8 ounce) package cream cheese, softened
2 tablespoons grated Parmesan cheese

Brie and Mango Quesadillas

1. Melt butter in large skillet. Layer mango, red onion and Brie on one half of one side of each tortilla. Fold over tortilla. Sauté in pan until cheese is melted and tortilla is golden brown. Sprinkle outside of tortilla with cumin while browning. Garnish with avocado slices and cilantro. Cut tortilla into 4 to 6 slices. Serve warm. Yield: 16 to 24 servings.

3 tablespoons butter
1 mango, thinly sliced
1 small red onion, thinly sliced
⅓-½ pound sliced Brie
4 flour tortillas
cumin to taste

Brie in Pastry

1 (8 ounce) package cream cheese
1 cup unsalted butter
1½ cups flour
  pinch of salt
6 tablespoons green chile peppers, chopped
2 tablespoons salsa
2 tablespoons cilantro, chopped
2 (8 ounce) rounds of Brie or Camembert

very good
12/98

3 hrs. before
serving

tried one with
apples.

1. Combine cream cheese, butter, flour and salt in food processor or blender until it forms a ball. Wrap in waxed paper and chill in the refrigerator for about 1 hour.

2. Mix the chiles with the salsa and cilantro. Divide dough into four pieces and roll each into a 10 inch circle. Trim neatly, saving extra dough to decorate top, if desired.

3. Place one round of cheese on one circle of dough. Sprinkle ½ of the chile mixture on top of the cheese. Top with another circle of dough and tightly enclose the cheese. Repeat procedure with the second round of cheese. Chill for 1 hour. Bake at 400 degrees for 10 minutes on a large cookie sheet; reduce the oven temperature to 350 degrees and continue baking for 20 minutes. Remove from oven and cool at room temperature for at least 1 hour. Cut into wedges to serve. Garnish with black olives and cilantro. Yield: 8 to 12 servings.

Omit the chile peppers, salsa and cilantro. Top cheese round instead with fresh cracked pepper and chopped parsley, then enclose the dough. Garnish finished baked cheese with red and green apple slices.

Tomato-Basil Hors d'Oeuvres

1. In food processor or blender, process ½ cup oil, 1 tablespoon vinegar, egg, seasonings and basil leaves. Slowly add remaining ½ cup oil (drop by drop), then 1 tablespoon vinegar.

2. Spread bread slices with Basil Mayonnaise. Toast lightly at 350 degrees. Can be done ahead. Put tomato slice on top of toasted bread. Drizzle a few drops of oil, balsamic vinegar, salt and pepper. Garnish with chopped fresh basil. Can be heated slightly to blend flavors, or serve as is. For open faced sandwiches, use same procedure with Italian rolls or French bread.

If mayonnaise fails (rarely!), start over with another egg and 1 tablespoon vinegar, then add the whole (failed) first mixture.

1   baguette of bread, sliced thin on the diagonal
1   recipe Basil Mayonnaise
    Roma tomatoes, sliced ¼ inch thick
    olive oil
    balsamic vinegar
    salt and pepper
    chopped basil for garnish

Basil Mayonnaise:
1   cup oil (½ cup vegetable oil and ½ cup olive oil)
2   tablespoons vinegar
1   egg
¾   teaspoon salt
½   teaspoon dry mustard
¼   teaspoon paprika
⅛   teaspoon pepper
1   whole bunch, or 1 cup chopped basil leaves

Self help books proliferate,
But, if you're seeking "self",
The quintessential volume
Is on your kitchen shelf.

Stuffed Red Potatoes

2 **pounds small red potatoes**
1 **(8 ounce) container sour cream**
¼ **cup dry buttermilk salad dressing mix**
¼ **cup finely chopped bacon, cooked**
   paprika
   parsley flakes

1. Microwave or steam potatoes until tender. Cool potatoes and cut in half or bite-sized pieces. Hollow out potatoes with melon baller.

2. Blend potato balls, sour cream, salad dressing mix and crumbled bacon until smooth. Add additional sour cream if mixture is too dry or stiff.

3. Stuff potatoes. Dust with paprika and parsley flakes. Bake in oven for 10 minutes. Serve warm. Yield: 16 to 20 servings.

1 ounce of crumbled blue cheese may be added or substituted for bacon.

Spaedinis

1 **(3 pound) eye round roast, frozen**
1 **(12 ounce) package mozzarella cheese, shredded**
1 **cup margarine (½ pound)**
3 **large containers seasoned bread crumbs**
   Romano or Parmesan cheese, grated
4 **large onions, quartered and sliced**
1 **cup vegetable or corn oil**
   skewers
   toothpicks

1. Have butcher thinly slice the frozen roast.

2. In the center of each slice of roast, place a pat of margarine, a few pieces of shredded mozzarella, a pinch of seasoned bread crumbs and a sprinkle of grated cheese. Roll up, tucking in sides so filling does not come out.

3. Place on skewers, alternating with onion pieces. Use approximately 6 pieces of meat per skewer. Dip skewer into oil and then into a tray of bread crumbs. Broil 5 minutes per side until golden brown. Remove from skewers and serve with toothpicks. Yield: 25 servings.

Cheese Rounds

1. In a medium bowl mix cheeses, seasoned salt, garlic powder and scallions. Add mayonnaise and increase as necessary to achieve a spreadable consistency.

2. Spread mixture on sourdough slices. Preheat broiler. Broil for 2 to 3 minutes. Serve at once. Yield: 60 servings.

1 cup shredded extra sharp cheddar cheese
¼ cup freshly grated Parmesan cheese
½ cup shredded mozzarella cheese
⅛ teaspoon seasoned salt
⅛ teaspoon garlic powder
4 scallions, diced
½ cup mayonnaise
1 loaf sourdough bread, thinly sliced and cut in half

Crisp Won Tons

1. Combine the pork, water chestnuts, scallions, soy sauce and egg. Mix well.

2. Place ½ teaspoon filling in center of each won ton wrapper. Dampen edges with water and fold on the diagonal, forming a triangle. Pinch together two farthest corners. Deep fry until golden.

3. To make the dipping sauce, mix together the vinegar and cornstarch. Add the remaining ingredients and cook slowly, stirring until thick and shiny. Yield: 80 to 90 servings.

1 cup ground pork, (¼ pound)
½ cup water chestnuts, chopped
3 tablespoons scallions, chopped
2 teaspoons soy sauce
1 small egg
1 package won ton wrappers, (3x3 inch size)
vegetable oil for deep frying

Dipping Sauce:
1 cup vinegar
2 tablespoons cornstarch
1 cup ketchup
½-1 cup sugar

Pesto Cheesecake

1	tablespoon butter
¼	cup dry bread crumbs
½	cup plus 2 tablespoons Parmesan cheese, grated
2	(8 ounce) packages cream cheese, softened
1	cup ricotta cheese
1	teaspoon salt
⅛	teaspoon cayenne pepper
3	large eggs
½	cup prepared pesto sauce
¼	cup pine nuts

1. Rub butter on bottom and sides of 9 inch spring-form pan. Mix bread crumbs with 2 tablespoons grated Parmesan cheese. Coat pan with mixture.

2. Blend cream cheese, ricotta, salt, cayenne and ½ cup Parmesan in large bowl until light. Add eggs one at a time. Beat well. Set aside ½ of the mixture.

3. Blend the other ½ with the prepared pesto sauce. Pour into the prepared spring-form pan, smooth the top. Carefully spoon the plain mix over the top, smooth. Top with pine nuts. Bake in a preheated 350 degree oven for approximately 45 minutes. Loosen sides, release spring, transfer to platter. Garnish with fresh basil sprig. Serve with crackers. Best served warm. Yield: 16 to 18 servings.

Tiny Cocktail Biscuits

1½	cups butter, softened
3	cups flour
3	cups crisp rice cereal
3	cups shredded cheddar cheese

1. Combine ingredients, mixing well. Shape into 1 inch balls. Bake at 375 degrees for 10 to 20 minutes. Biscuits become crisp when cooled. Yield: 9 dozen.

Provolone Pesto Loaf

1. Combine Pesto ingredients and puree until smooth. Set aside.

2. Combine Garlic Cream ingredients and puree until smooth. Set aside.

3. Line loaf pan with cheese cloth with excess hanging over sides and ends. Line the bottom and up the sides of the pan with ½ the provolone. Spread ½ the pesto on cheese. Layer ⅓ of the remaining provolone over the pesto. Sprinkle ½ the sun-dried tomatoes over the cheese. Spread all of the Garlic Cream over the tomatoes. Sprinkle with the remaining tomatoes. Cover with ½ the remaining cheese. Spread with last of the Pesto and cover with the remaining provolone slices. Fold cheesecloth over the loaf and press firmly. Refrigerate for 2 hours. To serve, unwrap and invert on platter. Garnish with edible flowers or basil. Serve with sliced baguettes. Yield: 20 servings.

1 pound provolone cheese, thinly sliced
½ cup oil packed sun-dried tomatoes, drained and chopped

Pesto:
3 cloves garlic
1 cup fresh basil leaves
1 cup grated Parmesan cheese
½ cup olive oil

Garlic Cream:
1 (8 ounce) package cream cheese, softened
¼ cup butter, softened
1 clove garlic, minced
¼ cup shelled pistachios, chopped

Salami Roll

1. Grind the salami, blend with the rest of the ingredients.

2. Cut off the ends of the baguettes, and cut each into 4 pieces.

3. With your thumbs, ream a hole in the center of the baguette. Stuff with salami preparation. Chill for 1 hour and slice. Yield: 6 to 8 servings.

1 (8 ounce) stick salami
1 (8 ounce) package cream cheese
1 (2¼ ounce) can chopped black olives
1 teaspoon Worcestershire sauce
¼ teaspoon hot pepper sauce
2 French bread baguettes

PRIZE WINNER • THE GREAT MONTEREY SQUID FESTIVAL

Squid Puffs

2½   **pounds cleaned squid**
1   **small onion**
3   **eggs**
1   **tablespoon chopped fresh parsley**
1   **bunch green onions, finely chopped**
1   **tablespoon granulated garlic**
1   **tablespoon MSG seasoning**
  salt and pepper to taste
  cracker meal as needed

1. Grind squid and small onion fine.

2. Add eggs and remaining ingredients except cracker meal. Mix thoroughly. Add cracker meal as needed to make thick paste.

3. Form into little balls and roll each in cracker meal.

4. Cook in deep fat until golden brown. Serve with tartar sauce or your favorite cocktail sauce. Yield: 120 puffs.

Olive Stuffed Cheese Balls

1   **cup shredded sharp cheddar**
¼   **cup margarine or butter**
¾   **cup flour**
⅛   **teaspoon salt**
½   **teaspoon paprika**
  dash cayenne
30   **pimento-stuffed green olives or 30 black olives, well drained**

1. Combine all ingredients except olives in blender or food processor and mix until soft dough is formed.

2. Take 1½ teaspoons of soft dough and roll around a well drained olive. Place on a well greased baking sheet. Chill in refrigerator until baking time.

3. Preheat oven and bake at 400 degrees for 10 to 12 minutes. They will be lightly browned on bottom. Cool on rack for 10 minutes and serve. May be served warm or at room temperatures. Yield: 30 cheese balls.

May be prepared 1 day ahead and stored in the refrigerator until baking time.

used green - O.K.
(TRy Black next Time.
can only have 1 or 2.
strong Taste)

24

California Punch

1. Combine syrup ingredients, place in saucepan. Cook over medium-low heat for 10 minutes. Strain; discard spices, cool, chill syrup in refrigerator. Combine with remaining ingredients in a punch bowl. Add ice cubes. Garnish with lemon slices, orange slices, and maraschino cherries. Yield: Makes 4½ quarts. Serves 24.

Syrup:
- 1½ cups water
- 2 cups sugar
- 2 sticks cinnamon
- 2 teaspoons whole cloves
- ⅛ teaspoon salt

Added Ingredients:
- 2 bottles Burgundy wine
- 6 cups cranberry apple juice
- 1 (12 ounce) bottle carbonated water

Special Christmas Wassail

1. Simmer first 6 ingredients for ½ hour. Strain. Add rum and serve. Yield: Makes ½ gallon.

- 1 pint cranberry juice
- 6 cups apple cider
- ¼ cup sugar
- 3 cinnamon sticks
- 8 whole cloves
- 1 tablespoon allspice
- 1 cup rum

Margarita Wine Punch

1. In a punch bowl stir together all liquid ingredients. Add ice mold and float lime slices.

2. Moisten and dip rims of glasses in salt if desired. Yield: Makes 3 quarts. Serves 20 to 25.

- 3 (6 ounce) cans frozen limeade concentrate, thawed
- 1 (6 ounce) can frozen lemonade concentrate, thawed
- 3 (750 ml) bottles dry white wine
- 1 liter lemon lime soda
- 1 quart ice mold
  lime slices
  salt, if desired

Apricot Sour Punch

1 **(46 ounce) can apricot nectar**
1 **cup fresh lemon juice**
1 **(750 ml) bottle apricot brandy**
1 **quart club soda**

1. Mix together and serve over ice. Yield: 18 servings.

Bloody Mary Mix

1 **(46 ounce) can cocktail vegetable juice**
½ **cup fresh lemon juice**
2 **tablespoons Worcestershire sauce**
2 **tablespoons hot sauce or 4 drops hot pepper sauce**
1 **teaspoon celery seed**
2 **tablespoons chopped fresh dill, or 2 teaspoons dried**
2 **cups vodka**

1. Mix and serve over ice. Vodka may be added by the individual serving, if desired. Yield: Approximately 16 servings.

Soups, Chilis & Stews

CALIFORNIA

Prune Festival ™

YUBA CITY

CALIFORNIA PRUNE FESTIVAL
P. O. Box 3006
Yuba City, CA 95992
(916) 673-3436

In September, the *California Prune Festival* offers something for the whole family. Seven stages of continuous entertainment bring forth some of the best in Jazz, Rock n' Roll, children's and cooking entertainers in the Sacramento Valley. The Prune Industry shines through the Festival and all its artists and their wares, the farmers' market, classic car show and much more.

Chilled Avocado Yogurt Soup

1. Blend avocado, yogurt and stock until smooth. Add salt, pepper, cayenne and garlic powder, blend again. Sprinkle with chopped chives and bacon. Chill at least 20 minutes. Yield: 4 servings.

"The Avocado Lovers' Cookbook", Joyce Carlisle; copyright 1985, Celestial Arts.

1   **large avocado, mashed**
½   **cup yogurt**
2   **cups chicken stock**
    salt to taste
1   **teaspoon white pepper**
    dash of cayenne pepper
    dash of garlic powder
1   **teaspoon chopped chives**
4   **slices bacon, cooked and crumbled**

Cold Strawberry Soup

1. Puree strawberries in blender, one package at a time.

2. Put the pureed strawberries into a large bowl. Add the sour cream, water, claret wine, lemon juice and salt.

3. Beat until smooth and well blended; chill.

4. To serve, top each bowl with a tablespoon of whipped cream. Makes about 2 quarts. Yield: 6 to 8 servings.

3   **(10 ounce) packages frozen sliced strawberries in syrup, defrosted**
2   **cups sour cream**
1   **cup water**
⅓   **cup claret wine**
2   **teaspoons lemon juice**
    a few grains of salt
    whipped cream

PRIZE WINNER • GILROY GARLIC FESTIVAL

Garlic Mushroom Soup

20 cloves fresh garlic, peeled
1½ pounds fresh mushrooms
4 tablespoons olive oil
2 cups toasted bread crumbs
1 bunch fresh parsley, stems removed, chopped fine
10 cups chicken broth
salt and pepper to taste
dash hot pepper sauce
dry sherry wine to taste, (optional)

1. Finely chop garlic and 1 pound of the mushrooms. Cut remaining mushrooms into thin slices.

2. In a 4 quart saucepan, heat 2 tablespoons of the olive oil and sauté garlic and mushrooms for 3 minutes. Remove from pan and set aside.

3. Sauté bread crumbs in remaining oil. Add garlic and mushroom mixture to crumbs, stir in parsley and sauté for 5 minutes. Add broth and simmer, stirring frequently for 15 minutes. Season to taste with salt, pepper, hot pepper sauce and dry sherry if desired. Yield: 8 to 10 servings.

If a thicker soup is desired, stir in a few teaspoons of cornstarch dissolved in a little cold water and simmer for a few minutes until soup clears and thickens.

**J. O. Manis
Courtesy of the Gilroy Garlic
Festival "Garlic Lovers
Cookbooks."**

Red Bell Pepper Soup

1. Cut unpeeled potatoes, place in a saucepan with the chicken broth. Bring to a boil, reduce heat, cover and simmer until potatoes are done.

2. Core, seed and cut red bell peppers into chunks. Peel and chop the onions. Peel and chop the garlic.

3. In a medium skillet, heat the olive oil, sauté the peppers, onion and garlic until onions and garlic are slightly brown.

4. Add sautéed pepper mixture to chicken broth and potatoes, then puree in a blender or food processor until very smooth.

5. Pour pureed mixture into a saucepan, stir in the half-and-half and season to taste with hot pepper sauce, salt and pepper. Heat over low heat. Do not boil. Garnish with a dollop of sour cream and fresh parsley. Yield: 6 servings.

4	cups chicken broth
½	pound red potatoes
2	tablespoons olive oil
1½	pounds red bell peppers
1	clove garlic
½	pound onions
1	cup half-and-half
	hot pepper sauce to taste
	salt and pepper to taste
	sour cream
	fresh parsley

Broccoli Soup

1. Chop broccoli into bite-sized pieces.

2. In a large pot, melt butter over medium heat. Add onion and cook 5 minutes. Add broth, potatoes, broccoli and carrots. Cover and simmer until potatoes are tender.

3. Puree the cooked mixture in batches in blender or food processor.

4. Return soup to original pot, reheat and serve. Yield: 8 servings.

1½	pounds broccoli
⅛	cup unsalted butter
1	medium onion, chopped
6	cups chicken broth
2	large white potatoes, cubed
4	carrots, thinly sliced
	salt and pepper to taste

Tomato Cheddar Soup

1 (16 ounce) can
   tomatoes, dice cut
1 (16 ounce) can tomato
   sauce
1 cup tomato juice
1 cup water
1 bay leaf
½ teaspoon salt
¼ teaspoon black pepper
¼ teaspoon garlic powder
1 tablespoon
   Worcestershire sauce
1 teaspoon sugar
1 cup shredded cheddar
   cheese
¼-½ cup sherry
   sour cream
   chives

1. Place tomatoes, tomato sauce, tomato juice, water, spices, Worcestershire sauce and sugar in saucepan. Bring to a boil.

2. Add wine and cheddar and simmer for 15 minutes. Garnish with a dollop of sour cream and chives. Yield: 6 to 8 servings.

Spicy Western Chile Verde

8 ounces or more diced
   round steak
1 tablespoon oil
3-4 cloves garlic, minced
1 teaspoon salt, or to
   taste
1 (4 ounce) can whole
   jalapeño chiles, diced,
   including seeds and
   ribs
1 (27 ounce) can whole
   green chiles, diced,
   including seeds and
   ribs
1 (27 ounce) can, filled
   with water

1. Sauté meat in oil until very well browned.

2. Add garlic, diced chiles, then water. Simmer about 30 minutes or until meat is tender and is the consistency desired. Serve with anything that needs to be moistened or needs additional flavor. It is great over eggs, with burritos, or over rice. Yield: 6 to 8 servings.

Tomato-Orange Soup

1. Cook tomatoes in small amount of boiling water until tender. Remove skin and puree.

2. Sauté onion and garlic in butter until golden brown. Add flour, stir and cook for 2 minutes.

3. In large saucepan, add tomatoes, stock, 1 cup of the wine and tomato paste. Add onions and cook on low temperature until reduced to half.

4. In food processor or blender puree orange, second cup of wine and ginger until smooth. Add to soup. Heat to simmering; stir in cream, salt and pepper to taste.

5. Soup may be served hot or cold. Serve garnished with a dollop of sour cream and chopped parsley and/or cilantro. Yield: 8 to 12 servings.

14 tomatoes
1 medium onion, minced
1 clove garlic, minced
3 tablespoons butter
3 tablespoons flour
6 cups chicken stock
2 cups white wine, divided
3 tablespoons tomato paste (if tomatoes need more taste)
1 orange, skin and all, cut into pieces
¼ teaspoon ginger
2 cups cream
salt and pepper to taste
sour cream
chopped parsley for garnish
chopped cilantro for garnish

Zucchini Soup

1. Wash zucchini and trim off ends. Cut into slices.

2. Heat butter or margarine in a Dutch oven. Add zucchini and chopped onion and sauté until limp but not brown (about 5 minutes). Add broth and simmer covered for about 15 minutes until vegetables are tender.

3. Pour into a blender a small amount at a time and whirl until smooth. Add cream, salt, pepper and nutmeg. Serve hot or cold. Yield: 4 to 6 servings.

5 medium-sized zucchini
¼ cup butter or margarine
1 medium onion, chopped
2 (14 ounce) cans chicken broth
½ cup half-and-half
⅛ teaspoon each salt and pepper
¼ teaspoon or less nutmeg

Black-eyed Pea Soup

1 (16 ounce) package
   dried black-eyed peas
1 large yellow onion,
   finely chopped
3 carrots, peeled and
   finely chopped
2 fresh tomatoes,
   chopped
1 cup ground smoked
   ham (ask butcher to
   grind a good deli ham)
2 stalks celery, finely
   chopped
2 cloves garlic, minced
1 cup Burgundy wine
½ teaspoon salt
½ teaspoon pepper
½ teaspoon ground
   coriander
1 quart chicken stock
   salsa
   sour cream
   green onions, chopped

1. Sort peas. Rinse. Add water to cover and soak overnight. Change water and cook 1 hour.

2. Sauté onion, carrots, ham, celery and garlic until softened. Add tomatoes, wine, peas, salt, pepper, coriander and stock. Simmer about 1 hour until peas are mushy. Puree, if desired. Thin with stock if necessary. Serve hot. Top with a tablespoon of salsa, a teaspoon of sour cream and a sprinkle of chopped green onion. Yield: 8 to 10 servings.

It is said that eating black-eyed peas on New Year's Day insures good luck for the coming year. This is a great way to get your dose.

Smoked Chicken, Corn and Black Bean Soup

1. On a covered grill, slightly smoke boneless chicken, cooking to medium rare (about 30 minutes). Use apple wood chips and do not allow the grill to become too hot or it will over smoke and over cook the chicken. (To save time you may purchase smoked chicken at your grocers.)

2. In ¼ cup butter sauté carrots, onion and celery for 5 minutes. Add thyme, oregano and basil; sauté 5 minutes more. Add wine and deglaze pan. Add hot chicken stock and reduce by one third. Add Worcestershire sauce, hot pepper sauce, smoked chicken, beans and corn. Simmer 5 minutes.

3. Add cream, simmer 5 minutes more and season to taste. (Thicken with cornstarch mixed with cold water if desired.)

4. Drop in remaining butter, piece by piece, stirring until melted. Garnish with cilantro if desired. Serve immediately. Yield: 12 servings.

1 cup diced smoked chicken
½ cup unsalted butter, divided
½ cup diced carrots
½ cup diced onion
½ cup diced celery
2 cups corn, fresh
2 teaspoons thyme
2 teaspoons oregano
1 teaspoon dried sweet basil
¼ cup dry white wine
4 cups chicken stock, hot
1 tablespoon Worcestershire sauce
½ teaspoon hot pepper sauce
1 cup cooked black beans
2 cups heavy cream
salt and ground black pepper to taste
2 tablespoons cornstarch mixed with a little cold water (optional)
fresh chopped cilantro for garnish

Super Bowl Clam Chowder

½ **pound bacon, diced**
3 **ounces Canadian bacon, diced**
2 **medium onions, diced**
3 **cloves garlic, minced**
4 **cups potatoes, diced**
1 **large carrot, shredded**
1 **stalk celery, finely diced**
2 **tablespoons dry parsley**
  salt and pepper to taste
1 **quart water**
2 **large tomatoes, diced**
4 **(7½ ounce) cans chopped clams, undrained**
1 **tablespoon lemon juice**
¼ **teaspoon hot pepper sauce**
1 **cup whipping cream**
  cornstarch, if desired

1. Fry bacon and Canadian bacon till crisp.

2. Add onion and garlic and cook, stirring until soft. Remove excess fat. Add potatoes, carrot, celery, parsley, salt and pepper. Add water to vegetables. Simmer 1 hour or until potatoes are soft.

3. Add tomatoes, clams and their liquid and lemon juice. Cook 1 hour on low heat. Add hot pepper sauce and whipping cream and heat but do not boil. May be thickened with equal amounts of cornstarch and water (mixed together) if desired. Yield: 6 servings.

In the sagas of sea and spray,
The story that wins the day
Is Jonah's tale
Of a giant whale—
"The big one that got away."

Clam and Corn Chowder

1. Drain clams.

2. In a large saucepan cook onions in margarine until tender. Add potatoes and clam nectar. Cover and simmer gently until potatoes are tender. Add corn and milk. Blend flour and melted margarine and stir into chowder. Cook slowly until mixture thickens slightly, stirring constantly. Add seasonings and clams. Simmer 5 minutes. Sprinkle with bacon bits and serve hot with oyster crackers. Yield: 6 to 8 servings.

Add hot pepper sauce or Cajun seasoning for a spicier flavor.

12	ounces chopped clams
1	cup or more clam nectar and water
1	tablespoon margarine
2	cups chopped onions
2	cups or more diced raw potatoes
20	ounces canned corn
3	cups milk
2	tablespoons flour
1	tablespoon margarine, melted
1	teaspoon celery salt
1	teaspoon salt
½	teaspoon white pepper
3	tablespoons bacon bits

Nutty Chicken Ragout

1. Season chicken with salt and cayenne pepper. Sauté chicken, onions and garlic in olive oil for 15 minutes.

2. Mix stewed tomatoes, peanut butter, tomato paste and chicken stock. Add to pan. Simmer, stirring constantly for 5 minutes over medium heat. Remove from heat and serve over rice or noodles. Yield: 4 to 6 servings.

8	boneless chicken breast halves
1	teaspoon salt
¼	teaspoon cayenne pepper
2	tablespoons olive oil
4	medium onions, chopped
3	cloves garlic, minced
2	(10½ ounce) cans stewed tomatoes
2	tablespoons tomato paste
3-4	cups chicken stock
1	cup extra crunchy peanut butter
1	cup chopped peanuts

Chicken Chili Stew

3 whole boned and skinned chicken breasts
2 tablespoons vegetable oil
1 large chopped onion
1 large green bell pepper, chopped
3 cloves garlic, minced
1 (28 ounce) can stewed tomatoes
1 (14 ounce) can pinto beans, drained
2 teaspoons chili powder
1½ teaspoons ground cumin
¾ cup picante sauce or salsa
salt to taste
chopped tomatoes
green onions
olives
grated cheese
sour cream
avocado

1. Cut chicken in 1 inch pieces.

2. Cook in oil, adding onion, bell pepper and garlic. Continue cooking until chicken turns white. Add rest of ingredients and simmer 20 to 30 minutes.

3. Serve with rice. Top with chopped tomatoes, green onions, olives, grated cheese, sour cream and avocado.
Yield: 4 to 6 servings.

May be used with flour tortillas as burrito filling.

White Chili

1. Soak beans covered with water for 1 hour. Drain beans, rinse and set aside.

2. In a large skillet place chicken breasts and 3½ cups water. Simmer, covered, for 30 minutes. Remove from skillet, reserve liquid and let cool. When chicken is cool, remove bones and shred meat.

3. Heat oil over medium heat in large pot. Add onions. Cook for 10 minutes. Add garlic, chiles, cumin, oregano, cloves and cayenne pepper and cook 2 minutes more. Add beans, stock and reserved chicken cooking liquid. Bring to a boil, cover and simmer until beans are tender, about 2 hours. Add salt to taste.

4. Stir in chicken and cheese and heat until chicken is heated and cheese is melted. Can be garnished with diced tomatoes, diced avocado, diced green onions, chopped cilantro and more shredded cheese. Yield: 6 to 8 servings.

2 cups dried small white beans
3 whole chicken breasts, skinned
3½ cups water
2 tablespoons olive oil
2 cups finely chopped onion
4 cloves garlic, minced
2 (6 ounce) cans diced roasted chiles
1 jalapeño chile, seeded and diced
2 teaspoons ground cumin
1 tablespoon fresh oregano, minced, or 1½ teaspoons dried
¼ teaspoon ground cloves
¼ teaspoon cayenne pepper
3 cups chicken stock salt to taste
2 cups shredded Monterey Jack cheese

PRIZE WINNER • CALIFORNIA PRUNE FESTIVAL

Prune Chili

3 pounds beef sirloin tip, cut into ½ inch cubes
½ pound sage or sweet Italian sausage links, casings removed
1 large onion, finely chopped
5 cloves garlic, finely chopped
12 ounces diced pitted prunes
1 (13¾ or 14½ ounce) can beef broth
3 cups water
1 (15 ounce) can tomato sauce
3 tablespoons California chili powder
3 tablespoons New Mexico chili powder
1 tablespoon jalapeño or Rio Grande chili powder
2 tablespoons ground cumin
1 tablespoon paprika
1 teaspoon dried oregano leaves
¼-½ teaspoon salt
shredded cheddar cheese
sliced green onion
diced tomato

1. In a 5 quart Dutch oven, sauté ½ of beef and ½ of sausage until well browned; remove to bowl. Repeat with remaining beef and sausage.

2. In same Dutch oven, sauté onion and garlic in beef and sausage drippings until they are golden. Stir in prunes and broth; heat mixture to boiling, stirring to loosen browned-on bits. Stir in browned meat and sausage, water, tomato sauce, the chili powders, cumin, paprika and oregano.

3. Heat chili to boiling over high heat. Reduce heat to low and simmer, covered, 2 hours or until beef is very tender, stirring occasionally. Season with salt and garnish each serving with cheese, green onion, and tomato, if desired. Yield: 8 servings.

You may substitute 3 tablespoons regular chili powder and 1 teaspoon ground red pepper for the combination of chili powders.

Rory Ramirez

He Man Chili

1. Brown beef quickly in small amount of oil. Set aside. Sauté onions in butter until tender. Add garlic and peppers and sauté until tender. Add green chiles and heat through.

2. Drain tomatoes but reserve liquid to use with cornstarch for thickener, if desired.

3. Put everything into a 6 to 8 quart pot except beef. Bring to a boil. If you want thicker chili, add cornstarch mixture. Return to boil then reduce heat.

4. Add browned beef to the pot. Season with salt and pepper to taste. Simmer briefly, covered. Serve with grated cheddar and Jack cheese, diced onions (red and white), hot tortillas, sour cream and any type of chunky salsa. Yield: 15 to 20 servings.

Place all ingredients in crockpot and cook on high for 6 to 8 hours.

3-4 **pounds top round steak, cubed**
2 **red onions, chopped**
1 **(4 ounce) can diced green chiles**
2 **large cloves garlic, minced**
1 **(28 ounce) can peeled tomatoes, drained**
1 **(28 ounce) can red kidney beans**
1 **(28 ounce) can pinto beans**
⅓ **cup chile powder**
1 **(8 ounce) can salsa de fresca (Mexican tomato sauce)**
1 **cup soy sauce**
1 **red bell pepper, chopped**
1 **green bell pepper, chopped**
½ **cup red wine**
½ **cup beer**

Chalupas

1 pound pinto beans
3-4 pounds pork roast, with or without bones
7 cups water
1 cup chopped onion
2 cloves garlic, minced
2 tablespoons California chili powder
1 tablespoon cumin
1 teaspoon oregano
2 (4 ounce) cans chopped green chiles salt to taste

1. Wash and sort pinto beans.

2. Trim as much fat from pork roast as possible.

3. Put all ingredients except salt into Dutch oven. Cover and simmer 5 hours, until meat falls apart and beans are done.

4. Pull meat apart, discarding any bones. Add salt, uncover and cook until mixture is thickened (about 30 minutes).

5. Serve on either flour or corn tortillas which have been heated, or over tortilla chips. Top with any combination of chopped tomatoes, onion, lettuce, avocado, shredded Jack or mild cheddar cheese, chopped cilantro, a squeeze of lime juice and the salsa of your preference. Yield: 10 to 12 servings.

This recipe is better the second day. It also freezes well.

Spicy Black Bean Soup

1. Soak black beans as directed on package.

2. Sauté onions, garlic and carrot in olive oil. Do not brown. Add broth, tomatoes and the rest of the ingredients to pan. Bring to boil and simmer 1½ hours or more until beans are tender.

3. Puree or serve as is, as you prefer. Top with sour cream and sherry, if desired. Yield: 8 to 10 servings.

1	pound black beans
2	large onions, chopped
3	cloves garlic, crushed
1	large carrot, chopped
¼	cup olive oil
8	cups chicken broth
1	(16 ounce) can diced tomatoes
1	teaspoon cumin powder
1½	teaspoons chili powder
1	chipotle chile, dried whole
½	tablespoon dried cilantro
½	teaspoon salt
⅛	teaspoon pepper
1	lime, juice only
1	ham hock
1	ounce Mexican chocolate, grated (or use 1 ounce unsweetened baking chocolate, 1 teaspoon sugar and ½ teaspoon cinnamon)

Veal Stew

1 clove garlic, minced
1 onion, coarsely chopped
4-6 tablespoons olive oil (divided)
2 tablespoons butter
4 carrots, coarsely chopped
1 large sprig rosemary
2 pounds veal, cubed, dredged in seasoned flour
1 cup white wine
1½ cups chicken broth
salt and pepper to taste
3 tablespoons chopped Italian parsley
1 head escarole, dark outer leaves chopped coarsely (saving white inside leaves for salads)
1 (10 ounce) package frozen baby peas, defrosted

1. Sauté garlic and onion in 2 table-spoons of the olive oil and the butter in a heavy skillet until golden. Add carrots and rosemary and cook until carrots are tender-crisp. Remove to bowl and set aside.

2. In same pan, add 2 to 4 table-spoons more oil and brown veal. Add wine and cook until the wine has almost evaporated, then add the chicken broth and salt and pepper to taste. Cover and simmer over low heat for 30 to 40 minutes until veal is tender. Add parsley, escarole and peas and cook over high heat until peas are heated through and escarole is wilted, but still bright green. Serve immediately. Yield: 4 to 6 servings.

Boeuf Bourguignon

1. Preheat oven to 350 degrees.

2. Brown beef well, about ¼ at a time, in 2 tablespoons hot butter in a large heavy skillet over moderately high heat; add butter as needed. Transfer browned beef to Dutch oven.

3. Heat 2 tablespoons brandy in small saucepan, ignite and pour over beef.

4. Sauté onions in 2 tablespoons butter in skillet, cover and cook, stirring occasionally, over low heat, until lightly browned. Add mushrooms, cook, stirring 3 minutes. Remove vegetables with slotted spoon to Dutch oven.

5. Blend cornstarch, beef extract and tomato paste in skillet. Stir in Burgundy, sherry, port and broth and bring this to a boil. Add pepper, bay leaf and remaining tablespoon brandy and mix well. Pour over meat and vegetable mixture in Dutch oven. Cover, put in oven and cook 1½ hours, or until beef is fork tender, stirring occasionally. Garnish with parsley and serve. Yield: 6 servings.

Even better made a day ahead, refrigerated and reheated gently, thinning with wine as needed.

2½ **pounds boneless stewing beef, cut in 1½ inch cubes**
4 **tablespoons butter (or more if needed)**
3 **tablespoons brandy, divided**
½ **pound small white onions, peeled (about 12)**
½ **pound small fresh mushrooms**
2½ **tablespoons cornstarch**
2-2½ **teaspoons beef extract**
2 **tablespoons tomato paste**
1½ **cups Burgundy**
¾ **cup dry sherry**
¾ **cup ruby port**
1 **(10½ ounce) can condensed beef broth, undiluted**
⅛ **teaspoon pepper**
1 **bay leaf parsley (for garnish)**

Hungarian Gabyassoup

2 pounds lean round steak, cut in small cubes
4-6 tablespoons oil, divided
3 large brown onions, chopped fine
3 large potatoes, diced
1 large tomato, peeled, seeded and diced
4 (14½ ounce) cans beef broth
4 teaspoons caraway seeds, crushed
1 teaspoon marjoram, dried
6 large cloves garlic, crushed
4½ tablespoons Hungarian paprika
salt and pepper to taste
3 tablespoons cornstarch (optional)

1. Brown beef cubes in ½ of the oil. Remove from skillet.

2. Add more oil as needed to lightly brown the onion. When the onion has turned golden, add the garlic, caraway seeds and marjoram. Stir to mix. Add beef, tomato, paprika and broth, still stirring. Salt and pepper to taste. Simmer 1 to 1½ hours.

3. Add diced potatoes and cook on low heat until potatoes are done, about 30 minutes. If thicker soup is desired, mix cornstarch with enough cold water to make a thin paste. Add to soup and stir until thickened. Yield: 8 servings.

There once was a dutiful daughter
Who cooked just the way her mom
  taught her;
But one day she read
A cook book instead,
And now branches out as she oughter.

Brunswick Stew

1. In a large kettle place pork chops, chicken breasts, lamb chops, sausage and steak. Add water and cook covered, 1½ hours or until meat is tender.

2. Strain stock into another kettle and refrigerate overnight. Remove bones from meat and cut into bite-sized pieces. Cover and refrigerate over-night.

3. Next day skim fat from the stock. Add tomato sauce, hot pepper sauce, vinegar, sugar, onions, garlic and tomatoes. Simmer, uncovered, for about 45 minutes. Add cream-style and kernel corn, reserved meat, chicken and sausage. Simmer for about 20 minutes or until meat is heated through. Stir in bread crumbs for thickening. Season with salt and pepper. Yield: About 7 quarts.

Great for post-Thanksgiving weekend; substitute leftover turkey for the chicken.

2   pork chops (about 1 pound)
2   whole chicken breasts
3   small lamb chops (about ¾ pound)
2   mild Italian sausages
1   pound round steak, cut into bite-sized pieces
6   cups water
1   (8 ounce) can tomato sauce
2   teaspoons hot pepper sauce (or to taste)
½   cup balsamic vinegar
½   cup sugar
2   cups chopped sweet or Vidalia onions
5   large cloves garlic, minced
2   (16 ounce) cans tomatoes with liquid, chopped
2   (16 ounce) cans cream-style corn
2   (16 ounce) cans whole kernel corn, drained
1   cup toasted bread crumbs, seasoned salt and pepper to taste

Cassoulet

2 pounds dry white beans
3 large onions, divided
9 large cloves garlic, minced, divided
1 teaspoon thyme, divided
4 bay leaves, divided
2 pounds lamb or beef, cut in stewing chunks
2 pounds goose or chicken, cut into pieces
2 pounds Polish sausages
  butter or olive oil
½ cup tomato sauce or 5 tablespoons tomato paste
2 cups white wine
  salt and pepper
2½ cups fresh white bread crumbs (no crusts)
¾ cup fresh chopped parsley

1. Cook beans according to package directions. Add 1 onion, 4 cloves garlic, ½ teaspoon thyme and 2 bay leaves.

2. Brown lamb and poultry in butter or olive oil. Remove from heat. Brown the remaining 2 onions. Add the remaining garlic, tomato sauce, thyme, bay leaves and wine. Salt and pepper to taste.

3. Cut sausage in half lengthwise, then into pieces. Brown sausage separately then add to lamb and poultry sauce.

4. To assemble, remove beans with a slotted spoon. Put ⅓ in casserole. Cover with a layer of lamb, poultry and sausage using a slotted spoon. Repeat beans and meat with beans last. Ladle the liquid from the meat sauce. Add bean liquid, if needed to cover the beans.

5. Spread bread crumbs and parsley on top. Place in a preheated 325 degree oven for 1 hour. Raise the temperature to 400 degrees for 20 to 30 minutes to brown the bread crumbs. Push crust into beans with back of spoon. Lower the temperature to 350 degrees until crust forms again (about 15 minutes). Yield: 12 to 15 generous servings.

Salads

FALLBROOK AVOCADO FESTIVAL
233-A East Mission Road
Fallbrook, CA 92028
(619) 728-5845

Fallbrook, the friendly village, is known as the Avocado Capitol of the World. In April, the *Avocado Festival* features guacamole and citrus pie contests, arts and crafts booths, animal shows, artist colony, wine tasting, Spanish Village and entertainment.

Cashew/Spinach Salad

1. Toss spinach and lettuce. Add all ingredients except dressing.

2. Mix dressing and toss with salad just before serving. Yield: 14 servings.

May add 2 cups fresh bean sprouts for added texture.

2 bunches spinach, cleaned and chopped

1 head red leaf lettuce, chopped

4 hard boiled eggs, chopped

½-¾ cup cashews

6 pieces cooked bacon, crumbled

½-1 (8 ounce) can sliced water chestnuts

Dressing:

1 cup oil

⅓ cup vinegar

⅓ cup brown sugar

1 teaspoon dry mustard garlic salt pinch of salt

Spicy Tidbit
"*Oh, Rosemary,*" *Cicely gushed;*
"*I notice Anise being rushed.*
But dating old Basil
Is always a hassle;
I fear, in the end, he'll be crushed."

Swiss Spinach Salad

2   **bunches spinach, cleaned, torn into bite-sized pieces**

2   **cups shredded Swiss cheese**

½   **pound mushrooms, sliced**

10   **strips bacon, crisply cooked, drained and crumbled**

2   **hard cooked eggs, chopped**

1   **large tomato, cut into 8 wedges for garnish paprika**

Mustard Vinaigrette Dressing:

¼   **cup white wine vinegar**

2   **teaspoons Dijon mustard**

1   **teaspoon tarragon leaves, crumbled**

¼   **teaspoon salt**

⅛   **teaspoon freshly ground black pepper**

¾   **cup vegetable oil**

1. Place spinach, cheese, mushrooms, bacon and eggs in large salad bowl. Chill until serving time.

2. In blender or food processor, combine the first 5 Mustard Vinaigrette Dressing ingredients and blend well. With the machine still running, very slowly add the oil in a steady stream. Store up to a week in a tightly-covered container in the refrigerator.

3. Just before serving, toss with dressing and serve, garnished with tomato wedges and sprinkled with paprika. Yield: 8 servings.

Sake Chicken Salad

1. Whisk all dressing ingredients together and refrigerate until ready for use.

2. Combine soy sauce, sake and ginger root in deep frying pan. Boil 5 minutes to make syrup. Add chicken. Simmer 8 minutes on each side. Remove from pan and place on cookie sheet. Bake 300 degrees for 15 minutes. Cool. Shred.

3. Deep fry saifun or rice stix.

4. When ready to serve, combine all ingredients except almonds and add dressing. Sprinkle almonds on top for garnish. Yield: 8 servings.

1 cup soy sauce
⅓ cup sake or sherry wine
2 slices fresh ginger root
4 chicken breasts
1 medium head lettuce, torn into bite-sized pieces
6 green onions, thinly sliced
¼ cup toasted sesame seeds
1-2 ounces saifun (bean thread) or 3 ounces Chinese rice stix, deep fried
3 tablespoons slivered almonds, toasted

Dressing:
4 tablespoons white sugar
½-1 teaspoon salt
4-8 tablespoons lemon juice (or 6 tablespoons rice vinegar)
½ teaspoon pepper
2 tablespoons sesame oil
3 tablespoons Chinese parsley, finely chopped

Carnival Pasta Salad

4 whole chicken breasts,
   cooked and chopped
2 cups seedless red
   grapes
1 cup snow peas
2 heads lettuce
1 large celery heart,
   chopped
7 ounces 1 inch cheese
   ravioli, cooked, drained
   and chilled
1 (6 ounce) jar artichoke
   hearts, drained
½ large cucumber, peeled
   and sliced
½ cup raisins
2 green onions, chopped
1 (11 ounce) can
   mandarin oranges,
   drained (optional)
1 kiwi, for garnish

Dressing:
⅔ cup mayonnaise
½ cup Parmesan cheese
⅓ cup fresh lemon juice
   salt and pepper to taste

1. Mix all ingredients with dressing. Serve on lettuce leaf and garnish with peeled and sliced kiwi. Yield: 4 to 6 servings.

French Summer Salad

1. Combine chicken, zucchini and mushrooms. Sprinkle with nuts and Roquefort cheese.

2. Whisk vinegar, mustard, salt and pepper. Slowly add olive oil and whisk.

3. Lightly toss salad and dressing and serve. Yield: 8 servings.

4 **whole chicken breasts, boned, poached, and julienne cut**

2 **fresh zucchini, julienne cut**

½ **pound fresh mushrooms, sliced**

¼ **cup nuts (walnuts, pecans or almonds)**

¼ **pound Roquefort cheese, crumbled**

Dressing:

6 **tablespoons Champagne vinegar**

1 **teaspoon Dijon mustard**
  salt and pepper to taste

1 **cup extra virgin olive oil**

Chicken Salad Kon-Tiki

1. Combine chicken, celery, coconut and chutney. Mix well. Toss with Curry Dressing.

2. Cut cantaloupes in halves. Remove seeds and fill cavities with salad or, if desired, spoon chicken salad on shredded lettuce and garnish with cantaloupe slices. Another way to present salad is to cover with dressing. Arrange 3 slices melon on top to form a crown and sprinkle with coconut. Yield: 4 servings.

Flavor of curry powder better if cooked in small amount of water or chicken broth to make paste and then cooled.

2 **cups cooked chicken breasts, diced**

¾ **cup crisp celery hearts, diced**

½ **cup freshly grated coconut**

4 **tablespoons chutney**

2 **cantaloupes**

Curry Dressing:

½ **cup mayonnaise**

½ **cup sour cream**

1 **teaspoon curry powder**

1 **teaspoon lime juice**
  pinch of sugar
  salt and pepper to taste

Curried Chicken Salad

4 **cups cubed cooked chicken**
1 **cup sliced celery**
1 **cup halved grapes**
2 **cups pineapple chunks, canned in own juice, drained**
1 **(5 ounce) can sliced water chestnuts, drained**
½ **cup slivered almonds**

Dressing:

1 **cup mayonnaise**
2 **tablespoons sour cream**
1 **teaspoon curry powder**
2 **teaspoons soy sauce**

For a Crowd:

24 **cups cubed cooked chicken**
6 **cups sliced celery**
6 **cups halved grapes**
12 **cups pineapple chunks, canned in own juice, drained**
6 **(5 ounce) cans sliced water chestnuts, drained**
3 **cups slivered almonds**

Dressing:

6 **cups mayonnaise (1½ quarts)**
12 **tablespoons sour cream (½ pint)**
2 **tablespoons curry powder**
¼ **cup soy sauce**

1. Chill chicken for at least 2 hours. Add remaining ingredients.

2. Mix dressing and combine with salad. Garnish with grapes, strawberries, kiwi and edible flowers. Yield: 8 servings, or 40 to 50 servings for a crowd.

Papaya Chicken Salad

1. Mix all Curry Mayonnaise ingredients in small bowl. Set aside.

2. Combine chicken, celery, nuts, raisins, green onion and chutney in medium bowl. Add Curry Mayonnaise to moisten and toss well. Add apples and mix gently.

3. Spoon into halves of papayas and serve on bed of lettuce. Yield: 4 servings.

2 small papayas
2 cups cooked chicken, cubed
1 large celery stalk, thinly sliced
¼ cup peanuts or cashews
¼ cup golden raisins, softened in warm water
1 whole green onion, thinly sliced
2 tablespoons mango chutney
5 tablespoons Curry Mayonnaise
1 small red apple, cored and chopped

Curry Mayonnaise:
3 tablespoons mayonnaise
1 teaspoon curry powder
1 teaspoon Dijon mustard
1 teaspoon fresh lemon juice
1 large garlic clove, minced

Chinese Crunch Salad

½ cup butter or margarine
2 packages ramen noodles
½ cup sesame seeds
1 (6 ounce) package slivered almonds, toasted
¼ cup red wine vinegar
½ cup oil
¼ cup sugar
1 teaspoon soy sauce
  salt and pepper
1 large napa cabbage, thinly sliced
6 green onions, sliced

1. Sauté noodles in butter until light brown. Drain on paper towel. Add sesame seeds and toasted almonds. Can be made ahead and stored in container.

2. Mix oil, vinegar, sugar, soy, salt and pepper. Toss cabbage and onions. Do not add noodle mixture until serving time. For a luncheon dish, add cooked chicken, pork or ham sliced thin. Yield: 8 to 10 servings.

Thai Cucumber Salad

1 cup white vinegar
1 cup sugar
½ teaspoon salt
2 cucumbers, sliced and quartered
½-1 red onion, thinly sliced and diced
  cilantro for garnish

1. Put vinegar, sugar and salt in a pot and cook for 10 minutes, bringing to boil. Cool.

2. Mix cucumber and onion in bowl. Garnish with cilantro. Cover with vinegar sauce. Test for sweet, sour and salt. Yield: 5 to 6 servings.

Spicy Noodle Salad with Peanut Dressing

1. Cook noodles in salted water al dente. Rinse under cold water. Place in bowl and toss with oil to prevent sticking.

2. Blend peanut butter and hot chicken broth in a food processor or blender. Add the remaining ingredients, blend. Adjust seasonings to your taste.

3. To assemble, place noodles in bowl. Add all the vegetables. Cut lettuce and cabbage in small pieces adding as much as you feel necessary. Pour dressing over salad and toss gently. Tastes best when allowed to sit at room temperature for a couple of hours. Yield: 8 to 10 servings.

½   **pound spaghetti**
2   **tablespoons vegetable oil**
1   **red bell pepper, slivered**
8   **scallions, sliced**
   bean sprouts (optional)
10   **mushrooms, sliced**
3   **zucchini, halved and sliced**
½   **bunch cilantro, chopped**
½   **head of Romaine**
½   **head of napa cabbage**
   sliced chicken, or shrimp (optional)

Peanut Dressing:
¼   **cup sesame seeds, toasted**
½   **cup peanut butter**
2   **tablespoons rice vinegar**
1   **tablespoon dry sherry**
2   **tablespoons chili sesame oil**
2   **tablespoons minced fresh ginger**
½   **cup chicken broth, heated to boiling**
½   **cup red wine vinegar**
2   **tablespoons soy sauce**
2   **tablespoons Chinese red chili sauce, or to taste**
2   **garlic cloves, minced**
1   **teaspoon salt**

Summer Chicken Salad

3   chicken breasts,
    cooked and shredded
1   pound spinach, rinsed
    and drained
1   (8 ounce) can water
    chestnuts
2   boiled eggs, chopped
¼   cup slivered almonds,
    toasted
½   cup cooked and
    crumbled bacon
Dressing:
1   cup oil
¼   cup rice vinegar
⅓   cup ketchup
2   tablespoons sugar
1   medium onion, grated
    salt and pepper to taste

1. Place salad ingredients in bowl.

2. Mix dressing ingredients. Toss with salad and serve immediately. Yield: 8 to 10 servings.

Cold Salad Oriental

3   tablespoons salad oil
4   green onions, chopped
1   teaspoon fresh ginger,
    diced
1   garlic clove, crushed
⅓   cup soy sauce
3   tablespoons honey
8   teaspoons crushed red
    pepper flakes, or to
    taste
2   cups cooked beef or
    pork, cubed
1   head napa cabbage,
    shredded
½   cup bean sprouts
½   cup pea pods
1   cup sliced radishes

1. In medium saucepan, heat oil over medium heat. Add green onions, ginger and garlic. Stir-fry for 2 to 3 minutes. Discard ginger. Remove from heat, add soy sauce, honey, red pepper; pour over meat in medium bowl. Cover and refrigerate 1 to 2 hours or overnight; stir occasionally.

2. To serve, arrange vegetables in salad bowl. Place meat and marinade in center. Toss to serve. Yield: 4 servings.

Provencale Potato Salad

1. Blend dressing ingredients.

2. Mix sliced vegetables, dressing and pimentos and let stand at room temperature for 2 to 4 hours. Serve with bacon and green olives as garnish. Yield: 6 to 8 servings.

8   **medium new potatoes, cooked and thinly sliced**
2   **large green peppers, thinly sliced**
1   **small red onion, thinly sliced**
½   **pound mushrooms, thinly sliced**
1   **(4 ounce) jar sliced pimentos**
4   **slices bacon, cooked, drained, diced**
    pimento stuffed green olives

Dressing:
¾   **cup olive oil**
3   **tablespoons red wine vinegar**
3   **tablespoons Dijon mustard**
1   **clove garlic, crushed**

Sunny Day Salad

1. Marinate artichoke hearts, carrots and olives in Italian dressing several hours or overnight.

2. Tear Romaine and head lettuce into salad bowl in bite-sized pieces.

3. Add onion, if desired. Add marinated vegetables, toss lightly with blue cheese dressing. Sprinkle with croutons. Yield: 8 to 10 servings.

1   **(14½ ounce) jar artichoke hearts, drained and cut in half**
1   **(16 ounce) can sliced carrots, drained**
1   **(6 ounce) can medium pitted ripe olives**
½   **head Romaine lettuce**
½   **head lettuce**
    Italian dressing
    blue cheese dressing
    croutons
    onions (optional)

Salad Niçoise

8-10	small red potatoes, cooked until tender and sliced ¼ inch thick, unpeeled
1½	pounds fresh green beans, cut 1½ inch length and cooked tender-crisp
1	(7 ounce) can water-packed tuna, drained
1	head butter lettuce
2	hard cooked eggs, quartered
2	tomatoes, cut into 8 to 10 wedges each
½	cup pitted ripe olives
1	tablespoon capers
1	(2 ounce) can anchovy fillets (optional)

Dressing:

1	cup olive oil
⅓	cup red wine vinegar
¼	teaspoon salt
	freshly ground pepper
2	tablespoons finely chopped parsley
2	tablespoons finely chopped chives

1. Combine oil, vinegar, salt, pepper, parsley and chives in a jar. Chill.

2. Cover potatoes with just enough dressing to coat slices, mix lightly, cover and chill 2 hours.

3. Cover beans with dressing also, cover and chill.

4. On a large, shallow platter, mound potatoes down the center. Arrange tuna and green beans on each side. Add a border of butter lettuce around the edge of the plate. Top with egg quarters, tomato wedges, olives and capers. Criss-cross the anchovy fillets over the top of the potatoes.

5. Pour remaining dressing over the entire salad and serve.

6. Salad can be prepared ahead and assembled at the last minute. Yield: 4 main dish servings.

Pasta Fresca

1. Cook pasta al dente, cool.

2. Combine pasta, tomatoes, mushrooms, red pepper, black olives, green onions, 2 ounces feta and 2 ounces pine nuts (sautéed in 2 teaspoons olive oil) and mix in a large bowl.

3. Blend dressing ingredients well with wire whisk, and pour over salad. Add remaining feta cheese and pine nuts on top. Chill. Yield: 12 servings.

1   pound mostaccioli noodles
4   ounces crumbled feta cheese, divided
2   large ripe tomatoes, diced
1   (8 ounce) box fresh mushrooms, sliced
1   (4 ounce) can sliced black olives
4   green onions, diced
½   cup pine nuts, divided
½   red pepper, diced

Dressing:
¼   cup red wine vinegar
3   tablespoons seasoned rice wine vinegar
½   cup oil
2   tablespoons fresh parsley (or 1 tablespoon dried)
¼   teaspoon freshly ground pepper
1   tablespoon lemon juice
½   teaspoon dried mustard
½   teaspoon garlic salt

Pasta Salad with Aioli Dressing

16 ounces mostaccioli
    noodles
2   cups mayonnaise
9   medium cloves garlic,
    crushed
2   tablespoons lemon
    juice
1½ tablespoons Dijon
    mustard
1½ cups fresh spinach, cut
    into 1½ inch strips
1   cup red pepper, cut
    into 1½ inch strips
½   cup green pepper, cut
    into 1½ inch strips
1   cup snow peas, cut in
    half
1   (6 ounce) can black
    olives, cut in half
3   (6 ounce) jars
    marinated artichoke
    hearts, drained
1   teaspoon salt
¼   teaspoon pepper

1. Cook pasta as directed on package, drain, rinse with cold water and drain well.

2. Combine mayonnaise, crushed garlic, lemon juice and mustard in food processor. Blend until smooth, set aside.

3. Combine pasta and vegetables, toss well. Add salt and pepper and dressing. Toss well to coat pasta and vegetables. Chill overnight if possible. Keeps well in refrigerator for 2 to 3 days. Yield: 10 to 12 servings.

Chef Joel Esperanza's Avocado Vera Cruz

1. Thaw shrimp under cold running water. Drain.

2. Mix together ketchup, mayonnaise, orange juice and lemon juice. Add tomatoes, onion, cilantro, vinegar, olive oil, salt and pepper. Add shrimp. Mix and adjust seasonings. Chill.

3. Cut avocados in half and remove pits. You may peel them if desired. Arrange avocados on beds of curly leaf lettuce. Spoon shrimp mixture into each avocado half allowing about 2 ounces shrimp per half. Garnish with single cilantro leaf and stem. Serve immediately accompanied by slices of fresh fruit. Yield: 12 servings.

El Jardin Mexican Restaurant

6   ripe avocados
1   (12 ounce) bag cooked frozen small shrimp
½   cup ketchup
1   tablespoon mayonnaise
¼   cup orange juice
2   tablespoons lemon juice
½   cup diced tomatoes
½   cup diced white onion
1   small bunch cilantro (¼ cup, chopped)
1   teaspoon seasoned rice vinegar
1   teaspoon olive oil
  dash salt
  dash white pepper
  curly leaf lettuce

Seafood Pesto Salad

1. Cook shrimp and scallops 3 to 4 minutes until just cooked.

2. Prepare cheese tortellini, al dente, drain and cool.

3. Combine olive oil, lemon juice, basil leaves, garlic and Parmesan cheese in blender. Toss all ingredients together and garnish with basil leaves. Yield: 8 to 10 servings.

1   pound shrimp, peeled and deveined
1   pound scallops
2   pounds cheese tortellini
½   cup olive oil
½   cup lemon juice
1   cup fresh basil leaves
1   clove garlic, minced
½   cup grated Parmesan cheese
  salt and pepper to taste
  basil leaves for garnish

Salads 65

Pacific Seafood Salad

1 cup chopped green pepper
½ cup chopped yellow onion
2 cups chopped parsley
2 cups mayonnaise
2 (7½ ounce) cans crabmeat, drained, or fresh if available
2 (4½ ounce) cans shrimp, drained, or fresh if available
8 ounces fresh cooked lobster
1 (6½ ounce) can chunk or solid pack tuna, drained
1 teaspoon Worcestershire sauce
1 teaspoon salt
pepper to taste
dash of hot sauce
potato chips for topping (optional)

1. Gently mix all ingredients, except chips. Refrigerate 1 hour.

2. Crush chips and put on top. Bake at 350 degrees for 30 minutes or until heated through. Can be made a day in advance as marinating improves the flavor. Yield: 6 servings.

You can make it, bake it, and serve it hot for supper. Make it, don't bake it, and serve it on lettuce for luncheon. Make it, bake it, serve it, and place remainder in refrigerator for a delicious leftover.

The phrase that rings in memory
Whenever good friends meet,
That universal paradigm
Is "Come on folks, let's eat."

Dilled Shrimp and Rice

1. Cook rice according to package instructions.

2. Combine vinegar, oil, dill weed, salt and pepper in jar and shake well. Pour 2 tablespoons of dressing over hot rice. Toss gently. Cover and chill.

3. Combine chilled rice, green onions, radishes and cooked shrimp. Toss with remaining dressing.

4. On the edge of a large platter, arrange the pea pods in spoke fashion. Spoon rice mixture into center. Before serving, squeeze lemon over salad. Garnish with fresh dill and green onions. Yield: 5 servings.

1   cup long-grain rice
¼   cup white wine vinegar
¼   cup oil
1   tablespoon dill weed
½   teaspoon salt
¼   teaspoon pepper
¼   cup chopped green onions
¼   cup sliced radishes
½   pound cooked shrimp
½   pound fresh pea pods, blanched
1   lemon
    fresh dill and green onions for garnish

Tabbouleh Salad

1. Boil 2 cups water and pour over bulghur wheat. Let stand 1 hour. Water will be absorbed.

2. Mix all other ingredients and add bulghur. Refrigerate until ready to use. This salad improves on standing several hours. Adjust seasonings. Yield: 6 to 8 servings.

1   cup bulghur wheat
¼   cup vegetable oil
¼   cup lemon juice (⅓ cup if recipe doubled)
    salt to taste
1   teaspoon pepper
½   cup parsley
½   cup chopped basil or mint
1   green onion, chopped
2   stalks celery, chopped
3   tomatoes, chopped

PRIZE WINNER • CALIFORNIA STRAWBERRY FESTIVAL

Grilled Lemon Pepper Shrimp and Strawberry Salad

16 jumbo shrimp, shelled and deveined
    juice ½ lemon
1½ teaspoons lemon pepper
    salt and cracked black pepper
5   cups mixed baby lettuce (or other red and green lettuce), torn
1   pint strawberries, hulled, cleaned, halved

Strawberry Poppy Seed Vinaigrette Dressing:
1   cup canola oil
2   teaspoons fresh, strained lemon juice
½   pint fresh cleaned strawberries
¼   teaspoon lemon pepper
¼   teaspoon sugar
    cracked pepper and salt (optional)
1   tablespoon poppy seeds

1. Blend vinaigrette ingredients together (reserve poppy seeds) in a blender and process until desired consistency.

2. Sprinkle the shrimp with lemon juice, lemon pepper, salt and cracked black pepper to taste. Brush both sides of the shrimp with the vinaigrette; set aside.

3. Prepare a hot fire. Thread shrimp on long metal skewers. Cook on an oiled grill set 4 to 6 inches from coals, turning once, until they are firm to the touch and opaque throughout, about 6 minutes (for quicker preparation, shrimp may be broiled).

4. Pour vinaigrette into a decorative container, add poppy seeds and whisk the ingredients together well.

5. Toss the baby lettuce lightly with some vinaigrette, just to coat. Divide in 4 and place on individual plates. Place 4 shrimp on each plate and garnish with strawberries; spoon a small amount of vinaigrette over each salad. Pass remaining vinaigrette separately. Yield: 4 servings.

Kathleen Boulanger

Curried Smoked Chicken and Wild Rice Salad

1. Blend dressing ingredients.

2. Toss chicken, wild rice, scallions and raisins with dressing to coat. Line platter with lettuce and spoon salad on top. Yield: 12 servings.

2½ cups cooked wild rice
6   whole smoked boneless chicken breasts, diced
1   bunch scallions, tops included
1   cup golden raisins
3   cups mâche (lamb's lettuce)

Dressing:

2   cloves garlic, crushed
3   tablespoons white wine vinegar
4   tablespoons lemon juice
1½ tablespoons curry powder
3   tablespoons bottled mango chutney
⅔   cup olive oil
¾   cup sour cream
3   tablespoons water
½   cup finely chopped coriander

Wild Rice Salad

1. Cook rice according to package directions. Drain well. Cool to room temperature. Spoon into large bowl, add chicken, grapes, water chestnuts and mayonnaise. Toss ingredients, cover and chill.

2. Just before serving add cashews. Serve on lettuce leaves or line a bowl with lettuce leaves and fill with salad. Yield: 6 servings.

1   cup uncooked wild rice
2   cups cooked chicken, cubed
1½ cups green grapes, halved
1   cup sliced water chestnuts, drained
¾   cup mayonnaise
1   cup cashews lettuce leaves

PRIZE WINNER • HAYWARD ZUCCHINI FESTIVAL

Zucchini, Wheat and Walnut Salad

1 cup uncooked bulghur wheat
½ cup olive oil
¼ cup balsamic vinegar
2 teaspoons minced garlic
1 tablespoon summer savory
1 teaspoon thyme
¾ teaspoon salt
¼ teaspoon black pepper
¼ cup minced fresh Italian parsley
4 cups diced zucchini (⅓-½ inch size dice), approximately 1 pound
1½ cups coarsely chopped walnuts

1. Bring 1 cup water to a rapid boil in a medium saucepan. Stir in bulghur. Cover pan and remove from heat immediately. Set aside for approximately 1 hour for bulghur to completely absorb liquid.

2. In the bottom of a large bowl whisk together oil, vinegar, garlic, summer savory, thyme, salt, pepper and parsley. Add diced zucchini, chopped walnuts and soaked and cooled bulghur to bowl. Mix gently. If desired, place in a serving dish edged with leafy greens for garnish. Yield: 6 to 8 servings.

Phyllis Ciardo

Lentil Salad

1 pound dried lentils
¼ teaspoon baking soda
1 teaspoon salt
Dressing:
3 shallots, peeled
½ cup red wine vinegar
½ teaspoon black pepper
2 teaspoons prepared Dijon mustard
1 tablespoon fines herbs
1 teaspoon oregano
1 cup safflower oil
1 red pepper, chopped
¼ cup chopped parsley

1. Soak lentils 6 hours or overnight with baking soda. Drain and rinse thoroughly. Return to pot. Add salt. Cover with water by 1 inch. Bring to boil. Lower temperature and cook 15 minutes, or until tender yet firm. Drain. Rinse.

2. In food processor or blender with motor running, add shallots. Mince finely. Stop motor. Add vinegar, salt, pepper, mustard, fines herbs and oregano. Combine. With motor running, add oil in a slow steady stream. Marinate lentil salad 6 hours before serving. Add red pepper and parsley when serving. Yield: 8 servings.

Celery Slaw

1. Mix sugar through vinegar with whisk. Add salt, paprika, pepper, salad oil and vinegar. Blend. Slowly stir in sour cream until thoroughly blended. Toss with vegetables and garnish as desired.

2. Cover with plastic wrap and refrigerate overnight. Toss again before serving. Yield: 8 to 10 servings.

May add mandarin oranges, raisins, pineapple chunks or favorite nuts.

3   **cups thinly sliced celery**
½   **cup shredded carrots**
1   **zucchini, shredded**
Dressing:
1   **tablespoon powdered sugar**
½   **teaspoon salt**
½   **teaspoon paprika dash pepper**
2   **tablespoons salad oil**
1   **tablespoon wine vinegar**
⅓   **cup sour cream**

Vicious Garlic Salad

1. Blend first seven ingredients in wooden salad bowl. Add the fresh mushrooms and toss lightly. Let mixture stand at room temperature 2 to 3 hours to marinate well.

2. When ready to serve, add romaine lettuce torn into bite-sized pieces. Toss gently. Yield: 4 to 6 servings.

Avocado or drained artichoke hearts may be used in addition to mushrooms for variety.

¼   **teaspoon dry mustard**
⅛   **teaspoon black pepper**
¼   **teaspoon salt**
2   **large cloves garlic, crushed**
2   **tablespoons fresh lemon juice**
¼   **cup olive or salad oil**
¼   **cup grated Parmesan cheese**
¼   **pound fresh mushrooms, sliced**
1   **head romaine lettuce, cleaned and chilled**

Cauliflower Salad

4 **cups sliced cauliflower**
1 **cup ripe olives, sliced**
⅔ **cup chopped green pepper**
½ **cup chopped pimento**
½ **cup chopped onion**
Dressing:
½ **cup oil**
3 **tablespoons lemon juice**
½ **teaspoon sugar**
3 **tablespoons white wine vinegar**
1 **teaspoon salt**
¼ **teaspoon pepper**

1. Pour dressing over vegetables and refrigerate for at least 2 hours before serving. Does not keep more than half a day. Yield: 6 to 8 servings.

Marinated Broccoli Almondine

1½ **pounds broccoli**
½ **cup toasted slivered almonds**
    pimento strips
Marinade:
½ **cup oil**
6 **tablespoons white vinegar**
1 **teaspoon minced garlic**
¾ **teaspoon salt**
¼ **teaspoon pepper**
½ **teaspoon tarragon, crumbled**
½ **teaspoon thyme, crumbled**
½ **teaspoon dry mustard**
⅓ **cup thinly sliced green onions**

1. Wash and trim broccoli. Separate into flowerets. Slice stems diagonally ¼ inch thick. Steam both in ½ inch boiling salted water for 3 to 5 minutes until tender-crisp. Drain.

2. Blend dressing ingredients. Mix with hot broccoli and toss. Cover and chill for at least 4 hours.

3. Lift broccoli from marinade and arrange on platter. Sprinkle with slivered almonds and garnish with pimento strips. Yield: 4 servings.

Black Bean Salad with Goat Cheese

1. Marinate the black beans, garlic, onion, spices, lemon juice and olive oil overnight.

2. Just before serving, mix with the red pepper strips, sprouts and goat cheese. Serve on a bed of salad greens. Yield: 4 to 6 servings.

- 1 (15 ounce) can black beans, drained
- 1 clove garlic, crushed
- ½ cup chopped onion
- ¼ teaspoon coriander
- 1 pinch cayenne pepper
- ½ teaspoon ground cumin
- ½ teaspoon chili powder
- ⅛ teaspoon black pepper
- ½ lemon, juice only
- 1½ tablespoons olive oil
- ½ cup bottled roasted red pepper strips
- 1 generous handful sprouts
- 4 ounces crumbled Montrachet goat cheese
  salad greens

Fiesta Salad

1. Mix all ingredients except cilantro in a large bowl, salt and pepper to taste. Cover and refrigerate.

2. Add cilantro just before serving. Yield: 8 to 10 servings.

- 2 (15 ounce) cans black beans, rinsed and drained
- 2 (16 ounce) cans corn, drained
- 1 (14 ounce) can hearts of palm, drained and cut into thin rounds
- 4 large tomatoes, diced
- 1 medium red onion, minced
- 1 tablespoon olive oil
- 3 tablespoons lemon juice
- 1 bunch of fresh cilantro, chopped

Frankly Fabulous Salad Dressing

1   **cup mayonnaise**
⅓   **cup salad oil**
¼   **cup ketchup**
2   **tablespoons sugar**
2   **tablespoons vinegar**
2   **teaspoons prepared mustard**
½   **teaspoon paprika**
¼   **teaspoon celery seed**
½   **teaspoon dill weed**
¼   **teaspoon pepper**
1   **medium onion, cut into quarters**
2   **ounces blue cheese, crumbled (can add more if desired)**

1. Place all ingredients except blue cheese in food processor or blender. Mix well. Pour into another container. Add blue cheese and stir.

This is a great salad dressing or dip for vegetables or crackers.

Green Goddess Salad Dressing

1   **clove garlic, minced**
½   **teaspoon dry mustard**
1   **teaspoon Worcestershire sauce**
3   **tablespoons tarragon wine vinegar**
3   **tablespoons minced chives or green onions**
1   **cup mayonnaise**
½   **cup sour cream**
¼   **teaspoon black pepper**
2   **tablespoons anchovy paste**

1. Mix all ingredients except anchovy paste. The anchovy paste should be added just before serving because it gets stronger as it sits in the dressing. Yield: 6 to 8 servings.

For a delicious salad, toss with lettuce mixed with at least ⅓ cup parsley.

Blue Cheese Dressing

1. Combine dressing ingredients and serve on your favorite salad greens. Yield: About 3 cups.

4 ounces blue cheese, crumbled
1 cup sour cream
1 cup salad dressing
½ cup buttermilk
¼ cup sherry
1 clove garlic, crushed
   cracked black pepper to taste
   hot pepper sauce to taste

Garlic Dressing

1. Mix in blender and refrigerate. Yield: Approximately 2 cups.

6 ounces mayonnaise
1 (10½ ounce) can beef consommé
2 tablespoons red wine vinegar
3-4 cloves garlic, crushed
1 tablespoon coarsely crushed black peppercorns
½ package unflavored gelatin

Parmesan Salad Dressing

1. Mix all ingredients and shake well until blended. Chill.

This dressing is a nice alternative to hot spinach salad dressing, and is delicious on lettuce also.

¾ cup salad oil
2 tablespoons Parmesan cheese
¼ teaspoon sugar
½ garlic clove, minced
⅛ teaspoon pepper
¼ cup fresh lemon juice
¾ teaspoon salt, or to taste

PRIZE WINNER • CALIFORNIA STRAWBERRY FESTIVAL

Strawberry Vinegar

**fresh whole
strawberries
white vinegar
sugar**

1. Fill a jar nearly full of rinsed whole strawberries. Do not hull. Cover them with white vinegar and seal jar. Let stand for 10 days. Strain.

2. Reserve liquid. Add 3 cups of sugar for each pint. Boil gently a few minutes. Cool and bottle for use.

The vinegar has a delicious strawberry flavor and a beautiful natural ruby color. A special gift to give at Christmas time.

Marilyn Nash

Raspberry Vinaigrette

½ **cup salad oil**
½ **cup raspberry vinegar**
½ **teaspoon salt**
  freshly ground black pepper
1 **tablespoon crème fraîche**
2 **teaspoons sugar (or to taste)**

1. Mix ingredients with whisk.

Add this dressing with ¼ cup pine nuts and ⅓ cup dried cherries to your favorite salad greens.

*They asked her to bring a salad;
She wanted to do it right;
She put a special dressing on,
And tossed and turned all night.*

Breads & Brunch

CALIFORNIA HERBFEST
31765 Kings Canyon Road
Squaw Valley, CA 93675
(209) 332-2909

Located at the Squaw Valley Herb Gardens 35 miles east of Fresno on Highway 108, **The California Herbfest** features a fabulous selection of herb plants, guest chefs demonstrating their specialties and great herbed food. Plan to attend in April.

SELMA RAISIN FESTIVAL
1802 Tucker Street
Selma, CA 93662
(209) 896-3315

In May, Selma, "The Raisin Capitol of the World", invites you to come and enjoy gourmet raisin food tasting, raisin rolling, a forklift rodeo, horseshoe competition, raisin baking, arts and crafts, entertainment and much more.

Pumpernickel Bread

1. Combine chocolate and warm mashed potatoes; set aside. In a separate bowl, combine rye flour, caraway seeds, salt, molasses and shortening. Mix in chocolate and mashed potatoes.

2. Proof yeast in water with sugar; add to dough mixture. Add whole wheat flour and knead 20 minutes. Place sponge (dough) in a greased bowl; cover and let rise until double, about 1 hour. Punch down and let rise again until double, 40 minutes.

3. Grease two 9 inch pie pans and sprinkle with cornmeal. Punch down dough and divide in half. Place in pans and let rise 1 hour. Preheat oven to 375 degrees. Bake 25 to 30 minutes. Cool on a wire rack. Yield: 2 round loaves.

Steve Pynes

½ ounce unsweetened chocolate
1 cup mashed potatoes (warm)
3 cups rye flour
2 tablespoons caraway seeds, slightly broken
3 teaspoons salt
¾ cup molasses
2 tablespoons shortening
1¾ cups water
3 packages active dry yeast
1 teaspoon sugar
4 cups whole wheat flour cornmeal

Mexican Cornbread

1. Mix all ingredients, except cheese, in order given.

2. Pour ½ of the mixture into a hot, well oiled 9x9 inch pan or iron skillet. Sprinkle ½ of the cheese on top. Add remaining batter mixture and sprinkle remaining cheese on top. Bake 1 hour in 350 degree oven. Yield: 6 to 8 servings.

Delicious with barbecue or other meats.

2 eggs
1 cup sour cream
1 cup cream style corn
⅔ cup salad oil
1½ cups white cornmeal
3 teaspoons baking powder
1 teaspoon salt
1 (4 ounce) can chopped jalapeños
1 cup shredded extra sharp cheddar cheese
2 tablespoons chopped bell pepper

Creamy Chive Rings

1 **package yeast**
¼ **cup warm water (110 to 115 degrees)**
1 **cup milk**
½ **cup butter, divided**
¼ **cup instant potato flakes**
⅓ **cup sugar**
1¼ **teaspoons salt**
1 **egg, beaten**
3¾-4¼ **cups all-purpose flour sesame or poppy seeds**

Filling:
1 **egg, beaten**
¾ **cup whipping cream**
⅓ **cup fresh or dried chives**
½ **teaspoon salt**

1. In a small bowl, mix yeast and warm water; set aside. In a saucepan, heat milk, ¼ cup butter, potato flakes, sugar and salt to 110 to 115 degrees. Cool. Stir in yeast and egg. Gradually add enough flour to make a stiff dough. Knead about 6 to 8 minutes, adding additional flour if necessary. Place dough in a greased bowl, turning once to grease top. Cover and let rise until doubled, about 1 hour.

2. Place all filling ingredients in the top of a double boiler and cook and stir until thickened. Cool.

3. Punch down dough and divide in half. Roll each into a 12x16 inch rectangle. Spread ½ the cream mixture on each half of dough. Roll up jelly-roll style, starting at the narrow end. Seal edges. Place on a greased cookie sheet, seam side down. Shape into a ring. Cut 1 inch slices almost through the roll. Lay slices flat. Melt remaining butter and brush the ring with it. Sprinkle with sesame or poppy seeds. Repeat for the other half. Cover rings and let rise until doubled, about 1 hour. Bake at 350 degrees for 20 to 25 minutes. Cool on a wire rack. Yield: 2 rings.

Sue Schwaber

Sweet Poppy Seed Bread

1. Mix all bread ingredients and pour into baking pans. Bake for 45 to 50 minutes at 350 degrees.

2. Pour glaze over breads while still warm. These loaves freeze well. Yield: Two 7½x11 inch cakes or 5 to 6 small loaves.

Small loaves take less time, check after 30 minutes.

3	cups flour
2	cups white sugar
1½	teaspoons salt
1½	teaspoons baking powder
3	eggs
1½	cups milk
1½	cups salad oil
1½	teaspoons vanilla
1½	teaspoons butter flavoring
1½	teaspoons almond flavoring
3	tablespoons poppy seeds

Glaze:
¼	cup orange juice
¾	cup sugar
½	teaspoon each: butter flavoring, vanilla, almond flavoring

Strawberry Nut Bread

1. Combine dry ingredients. Mix well. Combine eggs, oil, strawberries, and walnuts. Add to dry ingredients. Mix well.

2. Pour batter into two 9x5x3 inch greased and floured loaf pans. Bake at 350 degrees for 1 hour or until a toothpick inserted in the center comes out clean. Serve with strawberry cream cheese. Yield: Two 9x5x3 inch loaves.

Bread is better the second day. Also freezes well.

3	cups all-purpose flour
1	teaspoon baking soda
1	tablespoon cinnamon
1¾	cups sugar
3	eggs, beaten
1	cup vegetable oil
2	(10 ounce) packages frozen sliced strawberries, thawed, including juice
1	cup chopped walnuts

Lemon Bread

½ cup shortening
1 cup sugar
2 eggs, beaten
½ cup milk
½ teaspoon salt
1½ cups flour
1 teaspoon baking powder
½ cup chopped nuts (optional)
1 lemon rind, grated
Glaze:
¼ cup sugar
   juice of 1 lemon

1. Cream shortening. Add sugar, beating until light and fluffy. Add the 2 beaten eggs, milk, salt, flour, baking powder and nuts. Fold in lemon rind. Bake at 350 degrees for 55 minutes in a 9x5x3 inch loaf pan.

2. Combine ¼ cup sugar and lemon juice and spoon over loaf after taking from oven. Cool before cutting. Great served with pineapple cream cheese. Yield: 10 to 12 servings.

Sausage Bread

1 cup chopped onions
1 pound bulk sausage
⅓ cup grated Parmesan cheese
¾ cup grated Swiss cheese
1 egg, beaten
6 drops hot pepper sauce
½ teaspoon salt
¼ cup fresh parsley, chopped
2 cups biscuit mix
¾ cup milk
¼ cup mayonnaise
1 egg
1 tablespoon water

1. Sauté onion and sausage until brown and crumbly. Drain well. Add next six ingredients to meat mixture.

2. Combine biscuit mix, milk and mayonnaise. Mixture will be lumpy.

3. Place ½ of biscuit batter in greased 9x9 inch pan. Pour sausage mixture over batter and cover with remaining batter. Batter will not cover completely. Mix egg and water and brush on top. Bake 30 minutes at 400 degrees. Yield: 10 to 12 servings.

Apricot Muffins

1. Preheat oven to 400 degrees. Grease bottoms of muffin pans.

2. Sift flour with sugar, baking powder and salt into large bowl. Add orange peel and apricots. Mix milk, oil and egg; beat with fork to mix well. Make a well in the center of flour mix. Pour in milk mix all at once; stir quickly with fork just until dry ingredients are moistened. DO NOT BEAT. Batter will be lumpy.

3. Using ¼ cup measuring cup (heaping), quickly dip batter into muffin cups filling almost full. Bake 20 to 25 minutes or until golden and cake tester inserted in center comes out clean. Loosen and remove from pan immediately. Serve warm. Even better with apricot jam. Yield: About 3 dozen muffins.

Peter Goetz

4   cups sifted all-purpose flour
½   cup sugar
6   teaspoons baking powder
1   teaspoon salt
2   cups milk
⅔   cup salad oil or melted shortening
2   eggs, slightly beaten
4   teaspoons grated orange peel (fresh)
2   cups dried apricots, finely chopped

Carrot-Pineapple Bread

1. Mix dry ingredients together.

2. Beat together oil and sugar, add eggs combining thoroughly. Blend in vanilla. Add carrots and pineapple blending thoroughly. Stir in the dry ingredients, then the nuts.

3. Grease and flour 1 large and 2 small loaf pans. Bake at 350 degrees for 45 to 60 minutes. Yield: 1 large and 2 small loaves.

Freezes well.

1   cup vegetable oil
2   cups sugar
3   eggs, slightly beaten
3   teaspoons vanilla
3   cups sifted flour
1   teaspoon baking soda
1   teaspoon salt
2   teaspoons cinnamon
2   cups grated carrots
1   (13¼ ounce) can crushed pineapple in its own juice, (not syrup) and juice
1   cup nuts

Pumpkin Muffins

3	cups sugar
1	cup salad oil
4	eggs
1	(16 ounce) can pumpkin
3½	cups flour
1½	teaspoons salt
1	teaspoon cinnamon
½	teaspoon cloves
½	teaspoon nutmeg
2	teaspoons baking soda
1	teaspoon baking powder
1¾	cups raisins
1	cup chopped pecans

1. Sift dry ingredients, set aside.

2. Beat together sugar and oil. Add eggs, and pumpkin blending thoroughly. Add dry ingredients, combining thoroughly. Stir in raisins and nuts.

3. Grease muffin pans, or use paper liners, and fill ¾ full. Bake at 350 degrees for 15 to 20 minutes. Batter will keep for a few days in the refrigerator. Yield: 3 dozen regular or 9 dozen mini-muffins.

Muffins freeze beautifully.

Famous Blueberry Muffins

½	cup butter
1¼	cups sugar
2	eggs
2	cups flour
2	teaspoons baking powder
½	teaspoon salt
½	cup milk
2½	cups fresh blueberries, washed and drained
2	teaspoons sugar

1. Combine butter and sugar until fluffy. Add eggs one at a time. Blend.

2. Sift dry ingredients and add to creamed butter and sugar mixture, alternately with milk.

3. Mash ½ cup of blueberries and fold into mixture by hand. Add remaining whole berries and fold in gently.

4. Fill muffin tins ¾ full. Sprinkle sugar over each muffin. Bake at 375 degrees for 25 to 30 minutes or until golden brown on top. Cool 30 minutes. Yield: 12 muffins.

Banana Bran Muffins

1. Sift dry ingredients together and set aside.

2. Combine oil, cereal, milk, bananas and egg. Mix well and let stand for 2 minutes to soften cereal.

3. Add flour mixture to cereal mixture, stir in raisins.

4. Pour into 12 lined muffin cups. Bake until lightly browned at 400 degrees for 25 minutes. Yield: 12 muffins.

These freeze well.

1 cup all-purpose flour
1 tablespoon baking powder
¼ cup sugar
½ teaspoon salt
¼ teaspoon cinnamon
¼ teaspoon nutmeg
¼ cup oil
2 cups bran flake cereal
⅔ cup milk
⅔ cup mashed ripe bananas
1 egg, or 2 egg whites
½ cup California raisins

Surprise Oatmeal Muffins

1. Heat oven to 400 degrees; line muffin tins with paper cups.

2. Combine oatmeal and buttermilk. Add brown sugar, eggs and oil. Add remaining ingredients and stir until just moistened.

3. Spoon into paper cups ¾ full. Add 1 teaspoon preserves to each muffin and cover with batter to top of paper cup. Bake at 400 degrees for 20 to 25 minutes. Yield: 18 muffins.

2½ cups old fashioned oatmeal
2 cups buttermilk
1 cup brown sugar, firmly packed
1 cup oil
2 eggs
2 cups flour
1 teaspoon baking soda
2 teaspoons baking powder
¾ teaspoon salt
18 teaspoons raspberry, strawberry or grape preserves

Apple Muffins with Rum Sauce

2 **large apples, quartered**
1 **cup sugar**
¼ **cup butter, softened**
1 **egg**
1 **cup flour**
¼ **teaspoon salt**
1 **teaspoon cinnamon**
½ **teaspoon nutmeg**
1 **teaspoon baking soda**
Rum Sauce:
1 **cup heavy cream**
1 **cup powdered sugar**
½ **cup butter**
2 **tablespoons rum**

1. In a blender or food processor, chop the apples to a fine dice. Place in a separate bowl.

2. Blend the sugar and butter, add the egg. Sprinkle in the flour, salt, soda and spices and blend. Scrape the mixture into the bowl with the apples and mix.

3. Bake in well-buttered muffin tins for 25 minutes at 350 degrees.

4. Combine ingredients for the Rum Sauce and heat in a double boiler.

5. Place the warm muffin on a dessert plate and pour on the Rum Sauce.

6. Garnish with a raspberry and mint leaf. Yield: 6 to 8 muffins.

The muffins can be made ahead and frozen. Thaw and microwave before serving. The sauce can be stored for a few days in the refrigerator.

Popovers

6 **eggs**
2 **cups milk**
6 **tablespoons butter, melted**
2 **cups flour**
1 **teaspoon salt**

1. Preheat oven to 375 degrees. Put popover cups in hot oven with ½ teaspoon butter in each cup while mixing batter. When butter sizzles, pour in batter.

2. With electric mixer, beat eggs until frothy. Add milk and butter. Beat again to reach frothy texture. Slow mixer and add flour and salt. At high speed, mix until blended. Pour into popover cups with sizzling butter. Bake for 1 hour. Serve immediately. Yield: 8 popovers.

Apricot Raisin Scones

1. Combine flour with sugar, baking powder and salt. Cut in the margarine until mixture resembles coarse crumbs. Stir in eggs, milk and raisins, mixing until dry ingredients are just moistened.

2. With floured hands, pat ½ of dough into a greased 8 inch round cake pan, pressing dough up sides of pan about ¼ inch. Spread with jam. Top with remaining dough, spreading evenly.

3. Brush top with melted margarine and sprinkle with sugar-cinnamon mixture. Bake at 425 degrees for 20 to 25 minutes. Serve warm. Yield: 8 servings.

Stacy Ekberg

2	**cups flour**
2	**tablespoons sugar**
3	**teaspoons baking powder**
½	**teaspoon salt**
½	**cup margarine**
2	**eggs**
¼	**cup milk**
1	**cup raisins**
½	**cup apricot-pineapple jam**
2	**tablespoons margarine, melted**
¼	**cup sugar**
1	**tablespoon cinnamon**

Baking Powder Biscuits

1. Sift dry ingredients. Add milk and salad oil. Mix using spoon. Mixture may be sort of lumpy.

2. Drop on greased cookie sheet. Bake at 450 degrees for 10 to 15 minutes. Yield: Makes 4 shortcake biscuits, or 4 to 6 biscuits.

For shortcake, add an additional 1 to 3 tablespoons of sugar. Split, butter and fill and top with fruit.

1	**cup flour**
1	**teaspoon baking powder**
1	**teaspoon baking soda**
⅛	**teaspoon salt**
1	**teaspoon sugar**
½	**cup sour milk (any kind)**
2	**tablespoons salad oil**

Danish Puffs

1 **cup margarine or
  butter**
2 **cups flour**
2 **tablespoons cold water**
1 **cup boiling water**
1 **teaspoon almond
  flavoring**
3 **eggs**
2 **cups powdered sugar**
1 **tablespoon margarine**
4 **tablespoons cream**
1 **teaspoon vanilla
  flavoring**
⅛ **teaspoon salt**

1. Cut ½ cup margarine into 1 cup flour. Add 2 tablespoons water, mixing into a soft dough. Divide dough into 2 equal halves and press each half into a 12x13 inch oblong pan or an ungreased baking sheet.

2. Combine boiling water and remaining ½ cup margarine in a medium saucepan and bring to a boil. Add almond flavoring and remove from heat. Add remaining 1 cup flour all at once and blend. Add eggs, one at a time, beating well after each addition. Spread this mixture onto both oblongs, dividing equally. Bake at 400 degrees for 40 to 45 minutes.

3. Meanwhile, combine powdered sugar, 1 tablespoon margarine, cream, vanilla and salt. Beat until smooth. Frost cakes while still hot. Cut into strips and serve. Yield: 10 to 20 servings.

This pastry is best served warm on the day it is made. The bottom crusts can be done the night before, and refrigerated. The cream puff top is done the next morning.

*Why is the sun like a loaf of bread?
I'll bet you never guessed:
It rises in the "yeast", and then
Goes down behind the "vest".*

(adapted from original)

Apricot Coffeecake

1. In a medium bowl combine the flour, sugar, baking powder and salt. Cut in cream cheese, butter and shortening with a pastry blender or 2 knives until the mixture resembles coarse peas. Stir in milk.

2. Turn dough onto lightly floured board. Knead gently 15 to 20 times.

3. Place dough on waxed paper and roll to a 8x12 inch rectangle and then place rectangle on baking sheet.

4. Spread apricot preserves to cover ⅔ of the rectangle lengthwise. Sprinkle with walnuts.

5. Fold the third of the rectangle without preserves over the center and then fold again, making 3 layers of dough. Seal all the edges.

6. From folded edge, cut dough into 1 inch slices to within 1 inch of the opposite side. Twist the strips so that the cut side is up. Place on greased baking sheet.

7. Bake for 18 to 25 minutes at 400 degrees or until golden brown.

8. Remove from baking sheet and cool for 10 minutes before glazing.

9. Prepare glaze by combining the powdered sugar, milk and vanilla in a small bowl. Drizzle on warm coffeecake. Yield: 1 coffeecake.

2⅓ cups presifted all-purpose flour
2 tablespoons sugar
1 tablespoon baking powder
½ teaspoon salt
1 (3 ounce) package cream cheese, softened
6 tablespoons butter, softened
¼ cup solid vegetable shortening
½ cup milk
½ cup apricot preserves (or other favorite preserves)
¼ cup chopped walnuts
Glaze:
1 cup powdered sugar
2 tablespoons milk
¼ teaspoon vanilla

E WINNER • CALIFORNIA HERBFEST

Grilled Rosemary and Garlic Bread

2 **(6 inch) sprigs freshly cut rosemary**
2 **cloves elephant garlic vegetable oil**
1 **baguette for 6 to 8 butter**

1. Wash, stem and finely chop the rosemary leaves.

2. Peel and coarsely chop the garlic.

3. Sauté garlic and rosemary in light vegetable oil in cast iron skillet. When slightly crisp with edges browned, remove from skillet and set aside.

4. Lightly brown 1½ inch pieces of bread on both sides in skillet. Lightly spread butter on final side, and top with 1 teaspoon of rosemary-garlic. Yield: 6 to 8 servings.

Crab Pizza

1 **large prebaked Italian shell or pizza crust**
1 **cup shredded Swiss cheese**
½-¾ **cup mayonnaise**
1 **teaspoon lemon juice**
¼ **teaspoon curry powder**
¼ **teaspoon salt**
2 **cups crab, fresh or canned**
1 **tablespoon chopped green onion**

1. Mix all ingredients and pat on shell. Bake for 20 minutes in 400 degree oven.

2. Put under broiler for the last 5 minutes to brown. May be mixed the day before and spread on shell as needed. Yield: 4 to 6 servings.

Spanish Sandwiches

1. Sauté onions and garlic in olive oil until soft. Stir in other ingredients.

2. Cut rolls in half and scoop out both sides and fill, or cut off one end and scoop out inside and fill.

3. Wrap in aluminum foil and freeze or place in covered roasting pan and bake for 1½ hours at 225 degrees. Yield: 24 servings.

4 large onions
2 cloves garlic
1 cup olive oil
2 (7 ounce) cans diced green chiles
2 (2½ ounce) cans chopped ripe olives
6 hard boiled eggs
1 cup shredded cheddar cheese
1 (8 ounce) can tomato sauce
2 tablespoons vinegar
24 small sourdough or French rolls

Spinach-Cheese Quesadillas

1. In medium skillet combine spinach, onion, tomatoes, garlic, lemon juice and cumin. Cook over low heat until liquid is absorbed, about 5 minutes.

2. Transfer to a medium bowl. Add ¼ cup Monterey Jack cheese, ricotta cheese and cilantro. Season with pepper.

3. Divide and spoon filling on 2 tortillas. Sprinkle remaining ½ cup Monterey Jack cheese over filling. Place remaining tortillas over cheese.

4. Set nonstick pan (8 to 10 inch diameter) over low heat. Heat both sides of each quesadilla until lightly brown and cheese melts. Cut each quesadilla into 4 inch wedges. Serve warm. Yield: 4 servings.

4 corn tortillas (7 to 8 inch diameter)
1 large bunch spinach, stems removed, washed and patted dry
¼ cup minced green onions
½ cup chopped tomatoes
1 clove garlic, minced
2 teaspoons fresh lemon juice
½ teaspoon cumin
¾ cup shredded Monterey Jack cheese
3 tablespoons ricotta cheese
2 tablespoons minced fresh cilantro freshly ground black pepper to taste

PRIZE WINNER • GILROY GARLIC FESTIVAL

Garlic and Chili Relleno Soufflé

softened butter and dry bread crumbs for mold

5 **tablespoons butter, softened, divided**

3 **tablespoons all-purpose flour**

1 **cup hot milk**

¼ **teaspoon plus 1 pinch salt**

⅛ **teaspoon white pepper**

4 **large egg yolks, well beaten**

1 **(17 ounce) can peeled green chiles, drained and patted dry, cut in 1 inch pieces**

8 **cloves fresh garlic, minced**

5 **large egg whites**

½ **cup shredded Monterey Jack cheese**

1. Preheat oven to 375 degrees.

2. Grease a 1½ quart soufflé mold or pyrex baking dish generously with butter, and dust well with bread crumbs. Set aside.

3. Heat 3 tablespoons of the butter until it foams, add flour and cook over medium heat until it starts to brown, stirring constantly. Add hot milk and cook for 4 minutes, stirring constantly until thickened. Season with ¼ teaspoon of the salt and white pepper. Let cool slightly and add the beaten egg yolks, then the chiles and mix well.

4. Sauté garlic in remaining 2 table-spoons butter until golden brown. Add to the above mixture.

5. Beat egg whites with a pinch of salt until stiff. Fold beaten egg whites into first mixture then fold in the grated cheese. Pour into prepared mold and bake for 35 to 40 minutes until puffed and brown. Yield: 4 to 6 servings.

**Maria Sandoval
Courtesy of the Gilroy Garlic
Festival "Garlic Lovers
Cookbooks."**

Crustless California Quiche

1. Sauté mushrooms, celery and onion in butter until limp. Set aside.

2. Beat eggs and cream. Add flour, salt, paprika and pepper sauce. Beat well. Stir in ham, cheese and wine. Cover and chill.

3. Stir well and turn into a buttered 10 or 12 inch quiche dish or large deep pie plate. Bake in 350 degree oven for 50 to 55 minutes or until center is firm. Do not overcook. Let stand 10 minutes before serving. Yield: 10 servings.

It is best made ahead and refrigerated overnight. It can be served hot, warm or cold.

1 cup chopped fresh mushrooms, firmly packed in cup
½ cup finely chopped celery, firmly packed in cup
½ cup finely chopped green onion, firmly packed in cup
2 tablespoons butter or margarine
6 large eggs
1½ cups half-and-half cream
¼ cup flour
½ teaspoon seasoned salt
1 teaspoon paprika
½ teaspoon red hot pepper sauce
1 cup finely chopped cooked ham, firmly packed in cup (optional)
3 tablespoons dry white wine
1 cup shredded Swiss cheese, firmly packed in cup
1 cup shredded cheddar cheese, firmly packed in cup

No Crust Broccoli Quiche

4   medium eggs
6   tablespoons flour
½   teaspoon salt
⅛   teaspoon pepper
½   teaspoon dried thyme
2   cups cottage cheese
2   cups shredded sharp
    cheddar cheese
1   head fresh broccoli,
    chopped, or 1½ boxes
    frozen broccoli
    flowerets, chopped

1. Cook broccoli tender-crisp.

2. Beat the eggs. Add flour 1 tablespoon at a time. Add seasonings. Mix in cottage cheese and cheddar cheese. Add cooked broccoli.

3. Pour into a greased 10 inch deep-dish pie plate. Bake at 350 degrees for 45 minutes. Yield: 6 to 8 servings.

For the diet conscious, substitute low-fat cheeses, 1 carton of egg substitute for eggs, and add 1 teaspoon mustard for flavoring.

Egg and Cheese Casserole

10   eggs, beaten lightly
 2   cups whole milk
 1   teaspoon salt
 1   teaspoon paprika
 ¼   cup flour
 1   (3 ounce) can diced
     green chiles
 1   pint cottage cheese
1½   pounds shredded
     Monterey Jack cheese

1. Beat eggs lightly. Add the rest of the ingredients in the order given. Pour into 9x13 inch shallow baking pan. At this point it can be refrigerated overnight.

2. Bake at 350 degrees for 45 to 60 minutes, until set like a custard. Yield: 12 to 15 servings.

Wrapping the outside of the pan with aluminum foil acts the same as placing the pan in another pan of water. Also keeps the sides and bottom from becoming tough and too brown.

Cherry Pancakes

1. Combine Cherry Sauce ingredients in a saucepan and cook until thick and clear.

2. Mix dry ingredients and stir in eggs, milk and oil just until blended.

3. Pour batter onto a hot, greased griddle. Drop 5 to 6 cherries on each pancake. Turn cakes to bake other side. Sprinkle with powdered sugar or serve with cherry sauce. Yield: 8 to 10 servings.

2	cups flour
5	teaspoons baking powder
2	teaspoons salt
3	tablespoons sugar
2	eggs
2	cups milk
6	tablespoons oil
½-1	cup cherries (fresh, canned, dried, frozen sweet or sour)

Cherry Sauce:

1	cup cherry juice
1	tablespoon cornstarch
½	teaspoon salt
⅓-½	cup sugar
1	tablespoon butter
2-3	drops red food coloring

Hail to the popular brunch,
That marriage of breakfast and lunch;
It's all "tally-ho" for
The people who go for
The munch with the punch for
   the bunch.

Pictures
&
Menus

Sweetheart Brunch

Bloody Marys
or
Fresh squeezed California citrus juice

Turkey Breakfast Sausage

Egg and Cheese Casserole

Surprise Oatmeal Muffins

Popovers

Scrumptious Strawberry Dip

▲ ▲ ▲

A romantic meal for the one you love. The hearts, the flowers, a special card all come together to create a memorable occasion for just the two of you.

Spring Luncheon

Avocado Vera Cruz Salad

Smoked Chicken, Corn and Black Bean Soup

Grilled Rosemary and Garlic Bread

Indulge Today - Diet Tomorrow Trifle

▲ ▲ ▲

California flower fields are abloom. The colors are brilliant - the fragrance is intoxicating. Gather your friends and celebrate the season with a gala "salute to spring."

Mission Fiesta

Margarita Wine Punch

Ceviche

Brie and Mango Quesadillas

Aspararitos

Chili Relleno Casserole

Kahlúa Party Bars

▲ ▲ ▲

Since the days of the earliest Spanish settlers, missions and fiestas have been part of California's unique history. The fiesta, today, represents all-occasion celebrations to be enjoyed by everyone. So listen for the mariachis; join in the dancing; and add a spicy touch to the festivities.

Fourth of July Beach Picnic

Corn Dip

Holiday Dip

Marinated BBQ Steak

Provencale Potato Salad

Celery Slaw

Vicious Garlic Salad

Grandma's Apple Slices

▲ ▲ ▲

Bring your barbeque to the beach, and celebrate a typical California Fourth of July. Nibble on tasty appetizers. Savor cooked-to-perfection steak. Sample a trio of harmonious salads. Relish old-fashioned apple pie, but with a twist. Then sit back and enjoy the fireworks.

Vineyard View Dining

Artichoke Pâté

Red Bell Pepper Soup

Cashew/Spinach Salad

Chilean Sea Bass with Zucchini

Pasta in Garlic Oil

Strawberries in Mascarpone Cream

▲ ▲ ▲

Picture yourself dining al fresco at one of California's famous wineries. The sun is setting, and the colorful balloons hover over the vineyards as you sip vintage wine, relax and anticipate a splendid meal. Only a dream? Well, just treat yourself to the menu above, and part of your dream will come true.

Harvest Feast

Stuffed Clams

Zucchini Soup

Salad greens with Raspberry Vinaigrette

Cornish Game Hens with Apricot Almond Stuffing
and Grand Marnier-Currant Sauce

Make-Ahead Potatoes

Spinach-Artichoke Casserole

Brandy Pumpkin Pie

▲ ▲ ▲

Want to start a harvest tradition? Work your magic on this bountiful feast, and you will reap not only compliments, but long-lasting holiday memories.

Holiday in the Snow

Special Christmas Wassail

Prune Chili

Green salad with Blue Cheese Dressing

Mexican Corn Bread

Whiskey Bread Pudding

▲ ▲ ▲

Why not celebrate your holiday with a picnic in the snow? Chill the wine in a snow bank and savor the view as you ladle up steaming chili and call the snow bunnies to the table.

California born artist, Trudi Crockett, is known for her
unique watercolor card line of scenic resorts and
historical landmarks. With her familiarity and flair for
painting scenes of California, she has added an extra
ingredient of whimsical imagination to create all of
the illustrations for this cookbook.

Pasta, Rice & Grains

PASTA COOK-OFF/SAUSAGE CHALLENGE
P. O. Box 366
Weed, CA 96094
(916) 938-4624

In September the Weed Chamber of Commerce welcomes you to their annual
Pasta Cook-off/Sausage Challenge. This event features a craft fair, pasta
cook-off and tasting, spaghetti dinner and wacky meatball contest.

Risotto with Fresh Tomatoes, Basil and Mozzarella

1. Bring broth to simmer in saucepan.

2. In another 4 quart, heavy saucepan over moderate heat, sauté garlic, red pepper and onion in oil and butter for 1 to 2 minutes. Add tomatoes and sauté for 1 minute. Add rice and stir until well-coated. Add wine and stir until it is absorbed.

3. Begin to add the hot broth, ½ cup at a time, stirring frequently, until each addition of broth is absorbed. This takes approximately 17 to 18 minutes, by which time most of the broth has been added and rice is al dente.

4. Add last of broth and mozzarella, basil and Parmesan cheese. Stir to combine and melt cheese. Season to taste. Serve immediately in shallow, heated soup bowls. It seems a bit soupy at first, but continues to cook and absorb broth. Yield: 4 servings.

5	cups chicken broth
2	cloves garlic, minced
½-1	teaspoon dried, crushed red pepper
½	onion, minced
2	tablespoons unsalted butter
2	tablespoons olive oil
2-3	medium tomatoes, peeled, seeded and chopped
1½	cups uncooked Arborio (short-grain Italian rice found in Italian markets or specialty stores), or regular white rice may be substituted
½	cup white wine
4	ounces fresh mozzarella (packed in water) or packaged whole-milk mozzarella, cubed
½	cup fresh chopped basil
¼	cup grated Parmesan cheese
	salt and pepper to taste

Veal Risotto

Veal Sauce:
- olive oil
- 1 large veal shank
- 1 small onion, minced
- 1 carrot, chopped
- 1 stalk celery, chopped
- 1 red pepper, sliced thin (or diced)
- 1 sprig fresh rosemary
- 1 cup white or red wine
- 1½ cups chicken broth

Risotto:
- 1 tablespoon unsalted butter
- 2 tablespoons olive oil
- 2 cups Arborio rice
- 7-9 cups simmering chicken broth
- ½ cup orange juice
- ⅓ cup grated Parmigiano cheese
- chopped Italian parsley

1. Brown veal shank well in olive oil in sauté pan with lid. Set aside and brown vegetables in same pan. Add wine, stirring up browned bits. Cook over medium heat until reduced by half. Add broth, season to taste.

2. Add veal and rosemary. Cover and cook over low heat for 2 to 2½ hours until meat is very tender. Let cool. Remove meat from bone and cut into small pieces. Scoop the marrow from the bone and add marrow and meat to the sauce. Set aside. May be made ahead and reheated while rice is cooking.

3. For risotto, melt butter and oil in heavy saucepan. Add rice and stir to coat well.

4. Add broth ½ cup at a time, stirring well, until broth is absorbed. Test for seasoning. Stir frequently. Cook over medium heat for 18 minutes. Rice should still be al dente. Add veal sauce and orange juice and cook 2 to 3 minutes.

5. Remove from heat, stir in cheese and parsley. Serve immediately. Yield: 4 servings.

Wild Rice Casserole

1. Sauté onions in butter until tender. Add sausage and brown slowly. Add mushrooms and quickly brown. Drain drippings, reserving ¼ cup.

2. In a separate pan, heat reserved drippings. Stir in flour. Add cream. Cook until smooth and thickened. Add salt and pepper, bouillon cubes, sage and hot pepper sauce to taste.

3. In a large casserole combine wild rice, sausage mixture and all but ¼ cup of sauce. Top with remaining sauce. Bake 30 minutes at 350 degrees. Yield: 6 servings.

1 teaspoon butter
1 large onion, chopped
1 pound mild pork sausage
½ pound fresh mushrooms, sliced
¼ cup flour
2 cups light cream
½ teaspoon salt
½ teaspoon pepper
2 chicken bouillon cubes hot pepper sauce
¼ teaspoon sage
1 cup cooked wild rice

Spinach and Rice

1. Combine first four ingredients in saucepan. Sauté until onions are golden, (about 15 minutes). Add rest of ingredients. Mix.

2. Cover, bring to a boil, lower heat and cook 25 minutes, stirring occasionally. Remove bay leaves before serving. Yield: 6 servings.

Can be served hot or at room temperature.

¼-⅓ cup olive oil
2 medium onions, chopped
2 cloves garlic, minced
1 cup white rice
2 bay leaves
2 tablespoons tomato sauce
2 beef bouillon cubes
2 cups water
1 pound fresh spinach, washed, dried and chopped or 2 (10 ounce) packages frozen spinach, thawed and drained

Fettuccine with Walnuts and California Avocado

- 2 tablespoons olive oil
- ½ cup diced sun-dried tomatoes
- ¼ cup sherry wine vinegar
- ½ cup fresh chopped basil
- 2 tablespoons chopped green onions
- ¼ cup diced green bell pepper
- 2 tablespoons chopped walnuts
- 1 California avocado, diced
- 1¼ pounds dried fettuccine noodles (if not available, substitute any dried pasta)
  salt and pepper to taste

1. In a large bowl combine the olive oil, sun-dried tomatoes, vinegar, basil, green onions, bell pepper, walnuts and ½ of the California avocado. Toss ingredients well so they are evenly coated with the oil and vinegar.

2. Cook the pasta in boiling water for 3 minutes or until al dente. Drain pasta and pour into salad bowl with other ingredients while pasta is still hot. Toss all ingredients and serve immediately using the remaining California avocado as garnish on top of the pasta. Yield: 6 servings.

Recipe is courtesy of the California Avocado Commission in Santa Ana, California.

Tortellini with Tomatoes and Fresh Herbs

1. Using a large frying pan, heat the olive oil and add the shallots and garlic and cook until clear, not brown. Add the sliced mushrooms, cover and cook for approximately 5 minutes. Stir in the minced fresh herbs, pine nuts and tomatoes. Season to taste with salt and pepper.

2. Boil 4 quarts of water and add the fresh tortellini. Cook for 6 to 8 minutes. Drain the tortellini and add to the sauce. Serve and top with Parmesan cheese. Yield: 6 servings.

4 tablespoons olive oil
4 shallots, finely chopped
4 cloves garlic, minced
1 pound fresh mushrooms, sliced
10 leaves fresh basil, minced
1 tablespoon fresh marjoram, minced
1 tablespoon fresh parsley, minced
4 tablespoons pine nuts
2 (14 ounce) cans Italian tomatoes, sliced
   salt and pepper
5 cups fresh tortellini
   freshly grated Parmesan cheese

Pasta in Garlic Oil

1. Cook onions, shallots and garlic in oil. Add chicken broth and reduce to half.

2. Cook pasta al dente, drain. Just before serving add parsley and toss well. Yield: 6 servings.

A (7 ounce) can of chopped clams may be added.

½ cup olive oil
2½ cups chicken broth
1 large onion, chopped
4 shallots, chopped
8 cloves garlic, minced
1 cup fresh parsley, chopped
1 pound linguini

Tomato Broccoli Orecchiette

1½ cups canned chick-peas (garbanzo beans)
1 tablespoon olive oil, plus ¼ cup
1 head broccoli
½ pound orecchiette (or rigatoni) pasta
1 small red onion, diced
2 tablespoons finely minced garlic
2 cups fresh plum tomatoes, peeled and chopped (or canned, diced)
   salt and pepper
   Parmesan cheese (optional)

1. Mix the peas with 1 tablespoon olive oil.

2. Blanch the broccoli which has been cut into small flowerets in boiling salted water. Drain and refresh in ice water. Drain well.

3. Boil the pasta and cook al dente, about 12 minutes.

4. Heat ¼ cup olive oil in a 3 quart pan over medium heat. Add diced red onion and cook until tender. Add the chick-peas and garlic and cook until warmed through. Add tomatoes and broccoli and cook 2 to 4 minutes. Season with salt and pepper.

5. Drain pasta and add to pan, tossing to combine. Sprinkle with cheese, if desired. Serve immediately. Yield: 3 to 4 servings.

By offering pasta and rices
Embellished with sauces and spices,
You're upping the boodle
By using your noodle:
One of life's clever devices.

Pasta with Broccoli

1. Sauté garlic, onion, anchovy paste, pepper flakes and red pepper strips in olive oil 10 to 15 minutes over medium heat until tender. Add wine and reduce by half. Add chicken broth and parsley.

2. Bring salted water to boil and cook pasta according to package directions. Five minutes before pasta is cooked, add the broccoli and cook until both are al dente.

3. Drain in large colander and put in serving dish. Add the onion-broth sauce and 1 cup Parmigiano. Toss together to coat well and serve with additional cheese at the table. Yield: 8 servings.

2	tablespoons olive oil
2	cloves garlic, minced
1	onion, chopped
1	tablespoon anchovy paste
½	teaspoon dried red pepper
1	red bell pepper, thinly sliced
½	cup white wine
1	cup chicken broth
½	cup chopped Italian parsley
1½-2	pounds broccoli flowerets
1	pound penne or rigatonl pasta
1	cup Parmigiano cheese fresh black pepper

Cheesy Vegetable Lasagna

6 ounces lasagna
noodles cooked
according to package
directions

Tomato Sauce:
1 tablespoon oil
1 onion, chopped
6 ounces mushrooms,
sliced
1 small green pepper,
chopped
1 small zucchini, sliced
1 teaspoon dried basil
1 teaspoon dried
oregano
1 teaspoon salt
½ teaspoon pepper
2 tomatoes, peeled and
chopped
1 (15 ounce) can crushed
tomatoes
1 (5 ounce) can tomato
paste
½ teaspoon sugar

White Wine Sauce:
2 tablespoons butter or
margarine
2 tablespoons flour
2 tablespoons dry white
wine
1 cup milk
4 ounces cheddar
cheese, shredded

1. Tomato Sauce: Heat oil in pan, add onion, mushrooms, green pepper and zucchini. Cook and stir over medium heat until onion is tender. Add herbs, undrained tomatoes, tomato paste, tomatoes, sugar, salt and pepper. Bring to a boil, reduce heat, simmer uncovered 30 minutes stirring occasionally.

2. White Wine Sauce: Melt butter in pan, stir in flour, cook 1 minute, stirring. Gradually add wine and milk, stir over heat until sauce boils and thickens. Add cheese, stir until melted.

3. Spinach Layer: Heat oil in pan, add garlic, spinach and shallots. Stir fry about 3 minutes until liquid is absorbed.

4. Cheese Layer: Beat cheeses and eggs together until blended.

5. In a 9x13 inch glass pan, layer ½ of the tomato sauce, ½ of the lasagna noodles, the spinach mixture and the ricotta cheese mixture. Top with the rest of the noodles, the rest of the tomato sauce and cover with the wine sauce. Bake uncovered about 30 minutes in a 350 degree oven until top begins to brown. Let stand 10 minutes before cutting. Yield: 8 servings.

This dish freezes very well.

Spinach Layer:
1 **(10 ounce) package frozen chopped spinach, thawed and drained**
1 **tablespoon oil**
2 **cloves garlic, crushed**
2 **shallots, chopped**

Cheese Layer:
1 **pound ricotta cheese**
5 **ounces grated Parmesan cheese**
2 **eggs**

Pappardelle with Shrimp

1. Dissolve saffron in chicken broth, set aside.

2. Sauté garlic, shallots, basil and parsley in oil and season with peppers. Add chicken broth, wine and tomatoes. Cook for 15 minutes. Season to taste. Add evaporated milk.

3. Cook pasta al dente. Drain and put in serving bowl. Just before serving, put shrimp in sauce and heat through. Pour over pasta and serve. Yield: 6 to 8 servings.

2 **tablespoons olive oil**
2 **tablespoons chopped garlic**
¼ **cup chopped shallots**
¼ **cup chopped basil**
¼ **cup chopped parsley**
 white pepper
 red pepper flakes
1 **cup chicken broth**
 pinch of saffron
1 **cup white wine**
2½ **cups chopped tomatoes**
¼ **cup skimmed evaporated milk**
1 **pound cooked shrimp**
1 **pound pappardelle pasta**

Spinach Lasagna

1 (10 ounce) package
 lasagna noodles
1 (20 ounce) package
 spinach, washed and
 spun dry
2-4 cloves garlic
1 cup sliced mushrooms
2 cups chopped onion
10 ounces ricotta cheese
6 ounces feta cheese,
 crumbled
1 teaspoon each paprika,
 oregano, dried basil,
 black pepper
½ teaspoon salt
1 (26 ounce) can
 spaghetti sauce
2½ cups shredded
 mozzarella cheese
½ cup shredded cheddar
 cheese
½ cup grated Parmesan
 cheese
3 tablespoons olive oil
1 egg

1. Cook noodles ¾ recommended time and drain.

2. Place spinach in dry skillet over medium heat. Cover. Stir occasionally until all spinach is wilted. Set aside.

3. Sauté mushrooms, onion and garlic in olive oil over medium heat for about 10 minutes. Add ricotta, feta, cooked spinach and spices to onion mix. Heat through. Add the egg. Mix well.

4. In a lasagna dish, layer ⅓ of the noodles, 1 cup mozzarella, ⅓ of the spaghetti sauce, ½ of the spinach filling. Repeat. Top with remaining noodles, sauce, and remaining cheese. Cover and bake at 400 degrees for 45 minutes. Uncover and continue for 30 minutes or until cheese is browned on top. Let stand at room temperature for 15 minutes to set. Serve with rosemary garlic bread and crisp green salad. Yield: 8 servings.

Linguini with Garlicky White Clam Sauce

1. Melt butter in a pot. Add garlic and green onion and sauté until soft and golden.

2. Add garlic powder and flour to make a roux. Add clam juice and dry white wine. Cook until thickened. Add cream and stir until smooth. Simmer for about 10 minutes. Add clams and heat. (Do not cook clams for very long as they may toughen.)

3. Serve with linguini cooked according to package directions, and top with grated Parmesan cheese. Yield: 8 servings.

Jill Colombana

Clam Sauce:
- ¼ **pound butter**
- 1 **clove garlic, minced**
- ½ **teaspoon ground garlic**
- 2 **teaspoons garlic powder**
- 6 **green onions (white part only), thinly sliced**
- 6 **tablespoons flour**
- ½ **pint heavy cream**
- 2 **(7 ounce) cans chopped clams, juice too**
- 8 **ounces clam juice**
- 4 **ounces dry white wine**
- ½ **teaspoon salt**
- ¼ **teaspoon pepper (fresh ground white pepper preferred)**
- 1 **pound linguini**

White Clam Sauce with Spaghetti

¼ **cup butter or margarine**
1 **(8 ounce) package cream cheese**
2 **tablespoons dried basil**
2 **tablespoons dried parsley**
1 **clove garlic, minced**
⅓ **cup Parmesan cheese**
¼ **cup salad or olive oil**
⅔ **cup boiling water**
1 **(6½ ounce) can chopped clams, including juice**
¼-½ **pound sliced mushrooms**
1 **pound package spaghetti**

1. Melt butter and cream cheese. Add next five ingredients and mix. Add boiling water. Stir until smooth. Add clams and mushrooms. Heat through.

2. Cook pasta al dente.

3. Serve sauce over spaghetti. Yield: 5 to 6 servings.

Chicken Pesto

2 **cups fresh basil, firmly packed**
¾ **cup olive oil**
⅓ **cup pine nuts**
1 **clove garlic**
½ **cup freshly grated Parmesan cheese**
¼ **cup freshly grated Romano cheese**
1 **pound linguini**
2 **cups cubed cooked chicken**
salt and pepper to taste

1. In a blender or food processor puree basil, olive oil, pine nuts and garlic. Put into a mixing bowl. Add grated cheeses and mix.

2. Cook linguini al dente. Drain, saving 2 tablespoons of the hot cooking liquid. Add the liquid to the pesto. Stir.

3. Warm chicken.

4. Place linguini on serving plates, top with pesto, then with chicken. Serve immediately. Yield: 4 servings.

Cooked shrimp may be substituted for chicken.

The pesto may be prepared in advance and frozen.

Ravicotti

1. Defrost spinach and drain well. Squeeze out excess moisture.

2. Sauté meats with onions, garlic and parsley. Add salt, pepper and Italian herbs. Drain fat when meats are cooked. Cool. Add spinach, eggs and Parmesan cheese. Mix well. Fill uncooked manicotti tubes with mixture.

3. Pour enough of the spaghetti sauce in the bottom of a large rectangular baking dish to cover. Place manicotti on top of sauce leaving space between each tube. Add chicken broth so that it can be absorbed during baking. Put more spaghetti sauce on top. Sprinkle with grated cheese.

4. Bake in 350 degree oven for 1¼ to 1½ hours. Let sit for 10 minutes before serving. You may top with more sauce and grated cheese at this time. Yield: 14 servings.

This dish is called Ravicotti because it is a ravioli filling in manicotti tubes. It is a very rich dish and can be prepared ahead of time. Place the filled uncooked manicotti back in the original box, wrap box with a plastic bag and put in freezer until needed.

Jill Colombana

1	**pound ground chuck, ground round, or low-fat beef**
1	**pound ground turkey**
¼	**pound ground pork or a very high grade sausage**
1	**very large or 2 small onions, chopped**
2-3	**large cloves garlic, chopped**
2	**teaspoons dried parsley**
3-4	**eggs**
½	**cup grated Parmesan cheese (or more if needed)**
2	**(10 ounce) packages frozen chopped spinach**
1	**teaspoon Italian herb mixture**
1	**teaspoon salt**
½	**teaspoon pepper**
1	**quart spaghetti sauce**
1	**pound uncooked manicotti**
1	**(14½ ounce) can chicken broth**

Tagliatelle, Proscuitto and Mushrooms

1 **pound tagliatelle**
4 **tablespoons olive oil**
4 **cloves garlic, sliced**
½ **pound fresh mushrooms, sliced**
4 **ounces proscuitto ham, sliced wafer thin**
8 **ounces Parmesan cheese, grated, divided**
4 **ounces whipping cream**
2 **tablespoons pine nuts**
½ **teaspoon salt**
¼ **teaspoon pepper**
1 **teaspoon each, minced basil, marjoram, oregano and tarragon**
1 **pound tagliatelle**

1. Cook the pasta following the directions on the package. Do not overcook.

2. In a large pan, sauté garlic in the olive oil (do not brown), add sliced mushrooms and cover with lid. Steam until mushrooms are reduced to about ½ size.

3. Dice the proscuitto ham and add to the mushroom mixture. Add salt and pepper. When the ham is heated through (about 3 minutes) add ½ the Parmesan cheese, the pine nuts and the whipping cream. Continue to heat about 2 minutes.

4. Drain the pasta and turn into the large pan with the mushroom and ham mixture. Add the minced herbs. Sprinkle on the remaining Parmesan cheese. Serve at once. Yield: 4 servings.

Mary, Mary, culinary,
Are you a kitchen slave?
Heavens, no!
My status quo
Is having a microwave.

Pastitsio

1. Cook macaroni according to package directions. Drain and cool to lukewarm.

2. Spray large skillet with nonstick cooking spray. Brown meat until almost done, then add chopped onion and cook until golden. Stir in tomato paste and puree, salt, pepper and cinnamon. Bring to a boil and simmer, covered, stirring occasionally, for 30 minutes. Mix in bread crumbs.

3. Beat egg in large bowl. Add luke-warm macaroni and toss.

4. To make Egg White Sauce, melt butter in saucepan. Blend in flour, salt, pepper and nutmeg. Gradually add 2½ cups milk and cook, stirring, until smooth and thickened. Beat together the reserved ½ cup milk and the eggs. Stir into mixture and cook, stirring, over medium heat until slightly thicker.

5. In greased 9x13x2 inch baking dish arrange in layers ½ the macaroni, meat mixture, Egg White Sauce and Parmesan cheese. Repeat layers. Bake in preheated 375 degree oven 30 minutes or until golden. Let stand 10 minutes, then cut in squares. Yield: 8 servings.

8	ounces elbow macaroni
	nonstick cooking spray
1½	pounds lean ground beef
1	large onion, chopped
1	(10½ ounce) can tomato puree
1	(6 ounce) can tomato paste
1	teaspoon salt
¼	teaspoon pepper
¼	teaspoon cinnamon
⅓	cup dry bread crumbs
1	egg
1½	cups grated Parmesan cheese

Egg White Sauce:

⅓	cup butter
⅓	cup flour
½	teaspoon salt
¼	teaspoon pepper
⅛	teaspoon nutmeg
3	cups milk, divided
2	eggs

Roasted Tomato Sauce for Pasta

3 pounds Roma tomatoes
5 cloves garlic, peeled
1 bunch green onions
1 bunch Italian parsley or basil
  seasoned salt and pepper
  olive oil

1. Put tomatoes and herbs in large roasting pan, with herbs on the bottom. Drizzle with olive oil, season with salt and pepper.

2. Roast in 425 to 450 degrees oven for 45 to 60 minutes, until tomatoes are well browned. Let cool. Put everything in food processor and process until smooth. Depending on the thickness of the sauce, add chicken broth to thin, if necessary.

Makes a great summer sauce for pasta.

Veal Sauce for Pasta

½ ounce dried porcini mushrooms
  olive oil
3 pounds veal shanks
1 cup white wine
2 cloves garlic, minced
1 onion
2 stalks celery
½ cup fresh parsley
2 (28 ounce) cans tomatoes (crushed with added puree)
1 cup chicken broth

1. Soak porcini mushrooms in 1 cup warm water, strain and reserve water. Clean and chop mushrooms.

2. Brown veal shanks well in olive oil seasoned with salt and pepper. Set meat aside.

3. Chop garlic, onion, celery and parsley in food processor, then sauté in olive oil until tender. Add meat, tomatoes, broth, porcini mushrooms and add reserved water, salt and pepper and cook covered over low heat until meat is tender (2 to 2½ hours). Serve with farfalle (bowtie pasta), and with ricotta cheese and Parmigiano cheese at the table.

Chicken Sauce for Pasta

1. In a blender or food processor chop carrots, celery and onion. Set aside.

2. Brown chicken thighs in olive oil with anchovy and crushed red pepper. Deglaze pan with wine. Remove to bowl. Set aside.

3. Sauté chopped vegetables in olive oil until tender. Add tomatoes, water or broth, herbs and chicken. Cook over low heat until meat is tender. Serve with pasta, fresh Parmigiano, and chopped parsley or basil. Yield: 6 servings.

2 **carrots**
2 **celery stalks**
1 **onion**
   olive oil
6 **chicken thighs**
1-2 **anchovy fillets**
   crushed red pepper
1 **cup fresh parsley**
2 **(14½ ounce) cans crushed tomatoes with added puree**
1 **can water or broth freshly grated Parmigiano cheese fresh parsley or basil, chopped**

Polenta Baked with Onions

1. Cook polenta in double boiler with broth and salt, stirring occasionally, for 35 to 45 minutes, until thickened. Add cheese and test for seasoning.

2. Pour into well-greased 10x13 inch baking dish and top with caramelized onions. (Can be made ahead to this point.) Bake for 15 minutes at 400 degrees before serving. Yield: 12 to 15 servings.

Add 1 to 2 cups cooked or defrosted frozen corn before baking.

To caramelize onions, cook slowly in 1 tablespoon butter for 20 minutes or so until golden.

3 **cups polenta**
10 **cups broth**
2 **teaspoons salt, or to taste**
¾ **cup grated Parmigiano cheese**
2 **sliced onions, caramelized**

Baked Grains and Cheese

½ cup rice
½ cup bulghur
2 cups water
1 tablespoon olive oil
1 tablespoon butter or margarine
3 cloves garlic, minced
1 medium onion, chopped
2 stalks celery, chopped
1 serrano chile or other hot pepper, chopped (optional)
2 teaspoons each, cumin, coriander, dried oregano
1 teaspoon black ground pepper (or to taste)
¼ cup sour cream
1 green or red bell pepper, chopped
⅛ cup or 4 ounces chopped black olives
¼ cup Mexican salsa or Italian-style crushed tomatoes
1 egg
1 teaspoon salt, or to taste
1½ cups grated cheese (your favorite)

1. Put bulghur and rice in water. Bring to boil, cover and reduce heat to low. Simmer for 20 minutes (until water is absorbed).

2. Sauté garlic, onion, celery, bell pepper, serrano chile and spices for about 10 minutes in olive oil and butter. Leave pan on medium heat and mix in sour cream, rice, bulghur, mushrooms and olives. Stir. Add egg, salsa and ½ of the cheese. Stir. Cook for about 2 minutes.

3. Transfer to a 2 quart casserole dish. Top with remaining cheese and bake at 400 degrees for 20 minutes or until cheese is browned. Serve as a main course with a crisp green salad, or as a side dish. Yield: 4 main dish servings.

Seafood

HAYWARD ZUCCHINI FESTIVAL
P. O. Box 247
Hayward, CA 94543
(510) 581-4364

Eleven months out of the year, zucchini is just another common vegetable in Hayward but come August the unassuming squash is the guest of honor as approximately 40,000 zucchini worshippers flock to Kennedy Park to toast the diminutive, soft-skinned gourd. The Festival offers entertainment, arts and crafts, body building championship, vintage vehicle display and food.

THE GREAT MONTEREY SQUID FESTIVAL
2600 Garden Road, Suite 208
Monterey, CA 93940
(408) 649-6547

Memorial weekend is the time to attend *The Great Monterey Squid Festival*. This family event offers squid prepared a number of ways from fried to flamed. There are three outdoor stages with a variety of continuous entertainment, one outdoor stage just for kids, and an indoor seafood restaurant featuring Dixieland entertainment. Local and celebrity chefs offer cooking demonstrations. Indoor educational displays highlight the historic commercial fishing industry of Monterey. And there are a variety of arts and crafts.

Squid a la Binz

1. Preheat oven to 350 degrees.

2. Slice chiles lengthwise into pieces 2 to 3 inches long and ¼ inch wide. Cut cheese into finger-size pieces.

3. Stuff squid with 1 piece each of Jack cheese and green chile. Seal each with a toothpick. Layer squid on a baking dish. Sprinkle with salt and pepper, cover with tomatoes and lemon juice. Bake for 20 minutes.

3   pounds squid, cleaned and left whole
½   pound Monterey Jack cheese
1   large can whole mild green chiles
1   cup canned tomatoes, cut in half and drained
    juice of 2 lemons
    salt and pepper, to taste

Shrimp Florentine

1. Cook spinach. Drain and squeeze as dry as possible. Season with grated onion, lemon juice, salt, pepper and cayenne.

2. Make a cream sauce of butter, flour and cream. Blend in garlic, Worcestershire sauce, hot pepper sauce, paprika and sherry.

3. In a shallow casserole alternately layer the shrimp, spinach and cream sauce. Sprinkle Parmesan cheese on top. Heat in a 325 degree oven for about 30 minutes. Yield: 8 to 10 servings.

3   packages frozen chopped spinach
2   tablespoons grated onion
1   large lemon, juice only
    salt and pepper
    cayenne to taste
6   tablespoons butter
¼   cup flour
2   cups cream
2   cloves garlic, crushed
1   teaspoon Worcestershire sauce
3   drops hot pepper sauce
¼   teaspoon paprika
1   tablespoon dry sherry
2   pounds cooked shelled shrimp
    Parmesan cheese

Feta Shrimp Suprema

1	**(16 ounce) package rotelli pasta**
1¼	**pounds medium shrimp, cooked, shelled and deveined**
1	**pound feta cheese, rinsed, dried and crumbled**
6	**scallions, finely chopped**
4	**teaspoons chopped fresh oregano**
4	**Roma tomatoes, peeled, seeded and diced freshly ground pepper, to taste**

1. Cook pasta al dente. Cool. Combine all other ingredients. Toss lightly with pasta.

2. Refrigerate. Best if made day before. Yield: 4 to 6 servings.

The feta, shrimp mixture may also be made, brought to room temperature and served over hot pasta.

Shrimp Étouffée

2	**pounds fresh shrimp, peeled and deveined**
½	**cup butter or vegetable oil**
1	**cup finely chopped onions**
½	**cup finely chopped celery**
½	**cup finely chopped bell pepper**
4	**cloves garlic, pressed**
1	**tablespoon cornstarch**
1½	**cups water cayenne, to taste salt and black pepper, to taste**

1. Split shrimp and season generously with salt, black pepper and cayenne. Set aside.

2. Melt butter or oil and add onions, celery, bell pepper and garlic. Cook slowly in uncovered heavy pot until onions are wilted. Add seasoned shrimp and let simmer, stirring occasionally for 20 minutes.

3. Dissolve cornstarch in water and add to mixture. Cook another 15 minutes, stirring occasionally. Serve over rice. Yield: 4 servings.

Shrimp Stuffed Pepper Shells

1. Blanch peppers in microwave or in boiling water. Drain and set aside.

2. Sauté onions in butter or margarine until limp. Add flour and make a paste. Add sour cream, lemon juice, salt, pepper, Dijon mustard, parsley, shrimp, green chiles and curry if desired. Cook 5 to 7 minutes until thick and bubbly.

3. Fill pepper shells with shrimp mixture. Top with cheese. Bake 30 minutes at 350 degrees in a 9x13 inch baking dish. Yield: 8 servings.

4 **red or green peppers, halved and seeded**
6 **tablespoons butter or margarine**
½ **cup chopped onion**
6 **tablespoons flour**
1½ **cups low-fat sour cream**
1 **teaspoon lemon juice**
½ **teaspoon salt**
¼ **teaspoon pepper**
1 **cup low-fat shredded Swiss cheese**
2 **teaspoons Dijon mustard**
3 **tablespoons fresh chopped parsley**
1 **pound cooked bay shrimp, peeled**
1 **(4 ounce) can chopped green chiles**
1 **teaspoon curry (optional)**

The fishermen were sharing
Their tales of deep seafaring,
But Olaf missed
The salty gist
Cause he was "hard of herring."

Grilled Shrimp

½ cup canola oil
¼ cup red or white wine
¼ cup soy sauce
¼ cup lemon juice
2 tablespoons Worcestershire sauce
2 tablespoons red or white wine vinegar
1 tablespoon dry mustard
½ tablespoon paprika
1 clove garllc, minced
1 teaspoon red pepper flakes
2 pounds raw shrimp, shelled and deveined

1. Blend together marinade ingredients in a large bowl. Add cleaned shrimp and marinate at least 10 minutes, but no more than 30 minutes.

2. Drain marinade into a saucepan. Bring to a boil and simmer 3 to 4 minutes.

3. Skewer shrimp and grill or broil until pink and opaque in center, approximately 2 minutes per side. Serve hot marinade as a dipping sauce. Yield: 4 servings.

Leftovers are great served cold on a salad.

Seafood Quiche

2 tablespoons margarine
½ pound fresh mushrooms, thinly sliced
2 green onions, chopped
4 eggs
1 cup light sour cream
1 cup small-curd cottage cheese
½ cup Parmesan cheese
3 tablespoons flour
1 teaspoon onion powder
5 drops hot pepper sauce
2 cups shredded Monterey Jack cheese
1 cup crabmeat, drained
1 cup small cooked shrimp

1. Preheat oven to 350 degrees.

2. Sauté mushrooms and onion in margarine. Remove and drain.

3. In blender, combine eggs, sour cream, cottage cheese, Parmesan cheese, flour, onion powder and hot pepper sauce. Blend until smooth.

4. Pour mixture in large bowl. Stir in mushrooms, onions, Jack cheese and seafood.

5. Pour into 10 inch quiche dish. Bake 45 minutes or until knife inserted in center comes out clean. Let stand 5 minutes before cutting into wedges. Yield: 6 servings.

Scrumptious Shrimp Rémoulade

1. Combine Rémoulade Sauce ingredients in blender.

2. Halve avocados. Peel if desired. Fill avocados with shrimp.

3. Place on lettuce leaves on individual plates and garnish with deviled egg halves, tomato wedges, baby corn and parsley. Top with sauce and serve. Yield: 4 servings.

The sauce may be refrigerated and kept for 1 week.

2 **pounds cooked and peeled shrimp**
2 **large avocados**
  lettuce leaves
  deviled egg halves, for garnish
  tomato wedges, for garnish
  baby corn, for garnish
  parsley, for garnish

Rémoulade Sauce:
3 **tablespoons horseradish**
½ **cup hot mustard**
3 **cloves garlic, crushed**
1 **large onion, chopped**
4 **leaves celery, chopped**
2 **tablespoons paprika**
4 **sprigs parsley, chopped**
1 **cup salad oil**
2 **tablespoons Worcestershire sauce**
  salt and pepper, to taste

Seafood Soufflé

3 **eggs**
1½ **cups milk**
1 **tablespoon snipped fresh parsley**
½ **teaspoon dry mustard**
½ **scant teaspoon salt**
1 **heaping tablespoon "onion snow"**
1 **cup shredded sharp cheese**
8 **ounces crabmeat**
5 **slices of soft light bread, cubed**

1. Beat eggs until foamy.

2. Add next five ingredients and beat to mix.

3. Add cheese, crabmeat and bread cubes and toss lightly to mix.

4. Bake in ungreased 7½x11½ inch pan at 325 degrees for 45 minutes or until center is set. Yield: 4 servings.

To make "onion snow", freeze onion and grate finely.

An equal amount of imitation crab may be substituted.

Seafood Casserole

3 **cups mixed cooked shrimp, crabmeat and lobster**
¼ **cup chopped green onion**
¼ **cup chopped green pepper**
¼ **cup chopped pimento**
1½ **cups cooked rice**
1 **cup mayonnaise**
2 **tablespoons milk**
2 **teaspoons Worcestershire sauce**
1 **teaspoon lemon juice**
½ **teaspoon salt**
dash pepper
⅛ **cup Parmesan cheese**

1. Mix all ingredients except Parmesan cheese.

2. Turn into greased oven-proof casserole. Top with Parmesan cheese. Heat until bubbling. Can be prepared in advance and cooked just prior to serving. Yield: 4 to 6 servings.

Crabmeat Baked in Avocado

1. Preheat oven to 350 degrees. Cut avocados in half. Put crushed garlic and lemon juice inside. Let stand ½ hour. Discard juice and garlic. Set avocados aside.

2. To make Newburg Sauce, melt butter, stir in flour, salt and cayenne. When well blended add half-and-half and cook over low heat until sauce is smooth, just to boiling. Stir a little bit of sauce into egg yolks, add the rest of sauce bit by bit. Blend and add sherry.

3. Squeeze excess moisture from crabmeat and mix with celery and green onion. Add mixture to Newburg Sauce. Fold in egg whites.

4. Fill avocados with crab mixture. Sprinkle with bread crumbs and Parmesan cheese. Drizzle melted butter on top. Bake for 25 minutes. Yield: 8 servings.

4	ripe avocados
4	cloves garlic, crushed
2	lemons, juice only
6	cups Newburg Sauce
2	pounds crabmeat
½	cup chopped celery
¼	cup chopped green onion
5	egg whites, stiffly beaten
¼	cup melted butter
	grated Parmesan cheese
	bread crumbs

Newburg Sauce:

4	tablespoons butter
4	tablespoons flour
¾	teaspoon salt
	dash cayenne
2	cups half-and-half
4	egg yolks, well beaten
¼	cup sherry

I'm fond of seafood too;
And what I'd like to do
Is share a dish
Of charbroiled fish
And pick a bone with you.

Scallop Pasta Vigneron

3 cups dry white wine
¼ cup shallots, minced fine
¼ cup leeks (white part only), minced fine
3 cups heavy cream
8 ounces clam juice
1 cup Asiago cheese, grated
zest of 1 lemon, minced fine
¼ teaspoon cayenne pepper
8 ounces dried pasta (your choice)
1½ pounds bay scallops (the small ones)
1 cup fresh peas, blanched 1 minute in boiling salted water
3 tablespoons fresh chives, minced fine for garnish
2 tablespoons diced pimentos (if from a jar, rinse) for garnish

1. In a large, heavy-bottomed sauce-pan, bring the wine, shallots and leeks to a boil; reduce to 1 cup. Remove from heat, add cream, clam juice, Asiago cheese, lemon zest and cayenne. Return to heat, bring to a boil and stir constantly until the sauce is very thick. Reduce heat while you prepare pasta.

2. Cook pasta al dente. When pasta is done, increase heat under sauce and add scallops. Cook until scallops are just heated through (they overcook very easily).

3. Drain pasta thoroughly, toss with sauce and peas. Serve on warm plates. Garnish with chives and pimento. Yield: 10 to 12 servings as a first course; 6 to 8 servings as the main course.

Richard Nollevaux
Dry Creek Vineyards

Scallops Florentine

1. Preheat oven to 425 degrees.

2. Sauté mushrooms with butter and wine. Set aside.

3. Sauté minced garlic in butter or oil until golden. Add cream and reduce by half. Add spinach and seasonings, scallops, mushrooms and pasta and ½ the cheese.

4. Transfer to greased individual shell-shaped baking dishes and top with remaining cheese. Bake 10 to 12 minutes or until scallops are opaque. Serve immediately as first course. Yield: 8 servings.

2   tablespoons butter
2   tablespoons sherry or Marsala
2   cloves garlic, minced
½   cup butter or olive oil
1½ cups whipping cream
2   (10 ounce) packages frozen chopped spinach, defrosted and drained
¾   pound mushrooms, sliced
1   teaspoon salt
1   teaspoon grated nutmeg
½   teaspoon white pepper
2   pounds scallops, rinsed and drained
12 ounces shell pasta, cooked al dente, drained
3   ounces Parmigiano cheese, grated, divided

Oyster Pie

1. Mix all ingredients in a bowl.

2. Butter a 9x13 inch baking dish. Place the mixture in the baking dish and bake at 350 degrees for 45 minutes. Yield: 8 to 10 servings.

This recipe can be prepared the night before.

2   cups crushed saltine crackers
2   cups chopped fresh oysters
3   eggs, beaten
1½ cups milk
⅔   cup melted butter
    pepper to taste

Chilean Sea Bass with Zucchini

1½ **pounds Chilean sea bass fillets**
3 **cloves garlic, minced**
1-2 **tablespoons fresh cilantro, finely chopped**
2 **tablespoons oil-packed sun-dried tomatoes, drained and chopped**
2 **green onions, chopped**
1 **lime, juice only**
  dash of white wine
  salt and pepper
  paprika
2-3 **zucchini, sliced**
2 **tablespoons butter, melted**

1. Preheat oven to 450 degrees.

2. Arrange sea bass fillets in a single layer on a foil-lined pan.

3. Spread minced garlic, cilantro, sun-dried tomatoes and green onions over the fish. Squeeze the lime juice over the fish. Add a dash of white wine.

4. Arrange the zucchini around the sea bass fillets. Sprinkle the fish and zucchini with salt and pepper as desired and use the paprika sparingly to give the fish some added color. Drizzle the melted butter over the fish and zucchini.

5. Place another piece of foil on top and crimp foil all around the edges. Bake for approximately 20 minutes, or until cooked through. Yield: 4 servings.

Christine Nava

Lemon Soy Swordfish Steaks

⅓ **cup soy sauce**
1 **teaspoon grated lemon peel**
¼ **cup fresh lemon juice**
1 **clove garlic, crushed**
2 **teaspoons Dijon mustard**
½ **cup oil**
4 **large swordfish steaks**
  pepper to taste

1. Combine soy sauce, lemon peel, lemon juice, garlic, mustard and oil in bowl. Blend well.

2. Prick the fish to assure penetration of the marinade. Pour soy mixture over fish and refrigerate for 3 hours.

3. Broil or grill for 4 minutes on each side, or until done. Yield: 4 servings.

Fish with Vegetables in Papillote

1. Preheat oven to 350 degrees.

2. Place each fillet on a foil square. Atop each fillet put 1 tomato slice, 1 parsley sprig, 3 sliced mushrooms, 1 basil leaf, and 1 teaspoon lemon juice. Sprinkle with minced green onion and pepper. Lift end of foil and close tightly to make a pouch.

3. Set foil-wrapped fillets on a baking sheet. Bake 25 to 30 minutes. Fish may also be barbecued over a moderate fire. Serve fish in its pouch, steaming hot. Yield: 4 servings.

4 pieces aluminum foil, about 12 inches square
4 (5 ounce) sea bass, rock cod, or cabrilla fillets, thick and meaty
4 tomatoes, thickly sliced
4 sprigs parsley
12 fresh mushrooms, sliced
4 fresh basil leaves or 2 teaspoons dried basil
4 teaspoons fresh lemon juice
4 green onions, minced white pepper to taste

Swordfish in Parchment

1. Crush garlic into melted butter. Set aside.

2. To assemble, lay out parchment, put 6 spinach leaves on half of each sheet of parchment. Place swordfish steak on top of spinach. Divide peppers, squash and green onions over each steak. Top each with 2 tablespoons of garlic butter.

3. Rub some cold butter on edges of parchment. Fold top half of paper over the fish. Fold the edges together to form a sealed package.

4. Place on a jelly-roll pan. Cook at 450 degrees for 15 minutes. Fish and vegetables may be removed from or served in the parchment. Yield: 4 servings.

4 pieces of parchment paper, cut 8 by 12 inches, or use white paper bags
2 cloves garlic, crushed
8 tablespoons butter
4 small swordfish steaks, ¾ inch thick
¼ red or yellow pepper, julienned
1 small zucchini squash, julienned
3 green onions, finely sliced the same length as peppers and zucchini
24 large spinach leaves, rinsed and drained

Sicilian Style Swordfish

¼-⅓ **cup extra virgin olive oil**

4 **medium cloves garlic, whole**

2 **(35 ounce) cans Italian plum tomatoes, drained**

12 **small garlic cloves, thinly sliced**

¾ **cup sliced green olives with pimento**

½ **cup capers, rinsed and drained**

6 **(8 to 10 ounce) swordfish or shark steaks, 1 inch thick**

¼-½ **cup fresh Italian parsley, coarsely chopped**
dried red pepper flakes
fresh parsley, for garnish

1. Heat olive oil in heavy, large saucepan over medium heat. Add garlic cloves and stir until browned, about 3 to 4 minutes. Discard garlic. Add drained tomatoes. Increase heat and boil, crushing tomatoes. Boil for about 8 minutes until thickened. (This can be done 1 day ahead.)

2. Spread ½ tomato sauce on bottom of casserole dish. Top with ½ of sliced garlic, ⅓ cup olives and 2 tablespoons capers. Arrange fish on top. Cover with remaining sauce, then capers, garlic, olives and parsley. Sprinkle red pepper to taste.

3. Cover and bake at 350 degrees for 30 minutes if tomato sauce is hot. If tomato sauce is cold, bake 40 minutes.

4. Transfer fish to plates. Serve with rice. Use tomato sauce over all. Garnish with a bit of fresh parsley. Yield: 6 to 8 servings.

Honey Herbed Baked Salmon

1 **(6 to 8 ounce) salmon fillet per serving**

1 **teaspoon honey per serving**

1 **teaspoon fresh chopped basil per serving**
salt and pepper to taste

1. Rinse fillets and pat dry.

2. Place fillets, skin side down in a single layer on greased baking pan. Salt and pepper. Coat with honey and top with basil.

3. Bake for 15 minutes or until done, depending on thickness, ten minutes per inch. Serve immediately. Yield: 1 serving per fillet.

May substitute or combine marjoram, oregano, rosemary, dill or tarragon.

Red Snapper Fillets with Cream of Avocado Sauce

1. Marinate fillets in wine for 1 hour. Drain on paper towel.

2. Butter both sides of fillets. Sprinkle with paprika. Grill fillets 4 to 5 minutes each side or until fish flakes easily.

3. Sauté onion in butter until tender. Stir in flour and salt. Slowly stir in water. Boil for 1 minute. Remove from heat, stir in sour cream, horseradish and avocado. Heat gently.

4. Spoon sauce over fillets. Serve with lemon wedges. Yield: 4 servings.

"The Avocado Lovers' Cookbook", Joyce Carlisle; copyright 1985, Celestial Arts.

4   red snapper fillets
1   cup white wine
2   tablespoons butter
2   teaspoons paprika
Cream of Avocado Sauce:
2   tablespoons butter
2   tablespoons finely chopped onions
2   tablespoons flour
½   teaspoon salt
1   cup water
½   cup sour cream
2   teaspoons horseradish
1   avocado, peeled and diced

Saucy Strawberry Butter

1. Puree berries, ginger and rum in blender. In a medium-sized saucepan, melt butter over medium heat. Add flour and cook, stirring, for 1 minute. Add strawberry puree and cook, stirring, for 5 minutes more.

2. Spoon a portion of sauce over each serving of poached, broiled or grilled fish.

Niki LaMont

1   (8 ounce) package frozen strawberries, unsweetened
1   tablespoon crystallized ginger
1   ounce full-flavored rum
2   tablespoons sweet butter
1   tablespoon quick mixing flour for sauces and gravies

Barbecued or Baked Whole Salmon

1   (6 to 8 pound) dressed
     salmon
     salt and pepper
2   cups chopped fresh
     mushrooms
1   cup chopped green
     onion
2   tablespoons minced
     fresh parsley
½   cup grated Parmesan
     cheese
     grated peel and juice of
     1 lemon
½   cup butter, melted
4-5 lemon slices
Sauce:
½   cup butter
1   cup sour cream
¼   teaspoon seasoned
     salt or onion salt
1   tablespoon chopped
     chives
1   teaspoon fresh dill
     weed (optional)

1. Place fish on double thickness of heavy-duty foil, making sure foil is 3 to 4 inches longer than the fish at each end. Lightly salt and pepper the fish.

2. Combine rest of ingredients and spoon into cavity of fish.

3. Pour butter over fish and top with lemon slices. Seal foil. Place on grill, turning after 30 minutes. Cook another 30 minutes or bake in 350 degree oven until opaque, 10 minutes for each inch of thickness.

4. For sauce, melt butter in small pan over low heat. Stir in sour cream, salt, chives and dill weed if desired. Warm very gently, do not boil. Serve immediately. Yield: 10 to 12 servings.

Topping for Baked Fish

½   cup chopped green
     pepper
2-3 tablespoons margarine
2   cups fresh bread
     crumbs (4 slices)
½   cup mayonnaise
1   cup shredded cheddar
     cheese
1   tablespoon mustard
     salt and pepper to taste
1½   pounds fish fillets

1. Sauté green pepper in margarine until soft. Add remaining ingredients and blend well until cheese melts.

2. Spread mixture on fish fillets and bake until fish flakes easily with a fork and topping is slightly browned (approximately 25 to 30 minutes depending on thickness of the fish). Yield: 3 to 4 servings.

Poultry

DELICATO CHARITY GRAPE STOMP
12001 South Highway 99
Manteca, CA 95336
(209) 825-6212

In early September, celebrate the grape crush in the old tradition at the *Delicato Charity Grape Stomp*. Participants are given 90 seconds to "crush" as much juice as they can from a 25-pound lug of grapes which have been dumped into a large half-barrel. The juice yielded is then measured and the winners of each category recognized at the awards ceremony at the close of the event. Those attending will also be able to enjoy a car show, various arts and crafts booths, delicious food booths, wine related booths, Amateur Winemaking Competition, wine cooking demonstrations, entertainment and much more.

RIVERBANK CHEESE AND WINE EXPOSITION
3237 Santa Fe Street
Riverbank, CA 95367
(209) 869-4541

The Riverbank Chamber of Commerce welcomes you on the second weekend in October to the annual *Riverbank Cheese and Wine Exposition*. This two-day event features cheese and wine tasting sessions, a street festival with arts, crafts, antiques, food, live entertainment and a "Run for the Cheese".

Aspararitos

1. Cut chicken into short, thin strips. Cook bacon until done. Remove to paper towel; crumble. Pour off all but 2 tablespoons of the drippings. Cook and stir chicken and garlic in drippings until chicken is done. Stir in ½ cup picante sauce, beans, bell pepper, cumin and salt. Simmer until thickened, 7 to 8 minutes, stirring occasionally. Stir in green onions and reserved bacon.

2. Spoon bean mixture down center of each tortilla. Add 2 or 3 asparagus stalks; top with cheese and roll up. Place seam side down in lightly greased 9x13 inch baking dish. Spoon remaining sauce over top. Bake at 350 degrees for 15 minutes. Top with remaining cheese. Return to oven until cheese melts. Serve with chopped tomatoes, sour cream and additional sauce, if desired. Yield: 6 servings.

Debbie Rotert

1½ pounds asparagus, blanched
¾ pound boneless, skinless chicken breasts
4 slices bacon
2-3 cloves garlic, minced
1½ cups picante sauce
1 (17 ounce) can black beans, undrained
1 large green bell pepper, chopped
1 teaspoon ground cumin
½ cup sliced green onions
salt and pepper to taste
12 flour tortillas
1-1½ cups shredded Monterey Jack cheese

Chicken Breasts with Sweet Red Bell Pepper Sauce and Green Chili Salsa

6 boneless chicken breast halves
¼ cup lemon juice
salt and pepper

Sweet Red Pepper Sauce:
3 large red bell peppers
2 teaspoons peanut oil
2 tablespoons finely chopped onion
2 sprigs fresh thyme
¾ cup chicken stock
1 cup heavy cream
2 cloves garlic
salt to taste
lemon juice

Poblano Chili Relish:
2 medium poblano chiles
1 medium red onion, diced
2 cloves of garlic, finely chopped
1 tablespoon finely chopped fresh mint
1 tablespoon finely chopped green onion
1-2 tablespoons balsamic vinegar
2 tablespoons olive oil
½ tablespoon white wine
salt to taste

1. Salt and pepper chicken breasts to taste, and marinate in lemon juice.

2. Sweet Red Bell Pepper Sauce: Broil red peppers until evenly toasted. When cool enough, peel the skin off. Remove stem, seeds, and inner membranes. Cut into small pieces and set aside. Sauté onion and garlic in oil until transparent, add thyme and chicken stock. Cook until liquid is reduced by half. Add cream. In a blender combine roasted peppers and cream mixture. Blend until smooth. Season to taste with salt and lemon juice. Keep warm.

3. Poblano Chili Relish: Char, peel, seed, and cut chiles into a fine dice. Combine with the rest of the relish ingredients. Toss and let set at least an hour.

4. Barbecue the chicken breasts until done, approximately 15 minutes.

5. To assemble: put chicken breasts onto warmed plates, place ¼ cup of the warm pepper sauce over each breast, and top with the chili relish. Yield: 6 servings.

The Poblano Chili Relish can be made a day in advance and refrigerated.

Plum Wonderful Chicken

1. Mix together flour, salt & pepper in a bag. Add chicken and shake until chicken is coated. Heat oil in 10 inch fry pan. Brown chicken on both sides. Remove from pan.

2. Combine glaze ingredients in saucepan and heat until melted.

3. Place chicken into a 9x13 inch pyrex pan. Spoon glaze over chicken. Bake at 375 degrees for 45 minutes. Yield: 4 to 5 servings.

1   **cut-up fryer, or 6 thighs and 4 half breasts, skinless**
½   **cup flour**
1   **teaspoon salt**
¼   **teaspoon pepper**
¼   **cup canola oil**

Glaze:

1   **(10 ounce) jar plum jam**
2   **tablespoons ketchup**
2   **teaspoons lemon juice**
2   **teaspoons wine vinegar**
¼   **teaspoon hot pepper sauce**
½   **teaspoon allspice**
½   **teaspoon dry mustard**
¼   **teaspoon cinnamon**
½   **teaspoon ground ginger**
⅛   **teaspoon ground cloves**

People were coming for dinner;
And into the oven she looked;
There she saw nothing but ashes,
And knew her goose was cooked.

PRIZE WINNER • CALIFORNIA STRAWBERRY FESTIVAL

Grilled Young Chickens with Strawberry Marinade

4 **Cornish game hens
(1½ pounds each), split
fresh strawberries and
chopped mint leaves,
for garnish**
Strawberry Marinade:
¾ **cup pureed fresh or
frozen strawberries**
1 **cup strawberry vinegar
(see salad section)
grated zest of 1 lemon**
1 **tablespoon minced
shallot**
2 **tablespoons minced
fresh mint
freshly ground black
pepper, to taste**
⅓ **cup olive oil**

1. Combine the pureed strawberries, vinegar, lemon zest, shallot, mint and black pepper in a small bowl. Whisk in olive oil until well blended.

2. Place split chickens in a shallow glass or ceramic container and pour the marinade over them. Marinate at room temperature for 2 hours or in the refrigerator for about 4 hours.

3. Prepare a moderate charcoal fire in a grill with a cover. When the coals reach the glowing stage, remove the chicken from the marinade and place, skin side down, over the fire. Cover. Turn the chicken after 10 minutes and cook, basting frequently with the marinade, until the chicken juices run clear when pierced near the joint with a fork, about 25 to 30 minutes. Serve hot or at room temperature. Garnish with fresh strawberries and chopped mint leaves. Yield: 4 servings.

Vivian Ebert

Cornish Game Hens with Apricot Almond Stuffing and Grand Marnier-Currant Sauce

1. Rinse and pat dry hens, and season for baking.

2. Heat to boiling the apricots in 1 cup of the Grand Marnier, set aside.

3. Sauté onion and celery in ½ cup butter until limp. Put into a large bowl.

4. Cook sausage, drain and add to bowl with celery and onion mixture. Add apricots and Grand Marnier, stuffing mix and almonds.

5. Heat and mix remaining ½ cup butter and the chicken stock. Add remaining Grand Marnier. Combine with stuffing mixture. Add seasonings and stuff game hens. Bake at 350 degrees for 1 to 1½ hours.

6. Combine sauce ingredients and boil for 5 minutes. Pour some sauce over game hens to serve. Fill gravy boat with the extra sauce. Yield: 4 servings.

4 Cornish game hens

Apricot Almond Stuffing:
1 cup diced, dried apricots
1½ cups Grand Marnier, divided
1 cup melted butter, divided
1 large onion, chopped
2 cups coarsley chopped celery
1 pound spicy pork sausage
4 cups herb stuffing mix
1 cup slivered almonds or hazelnuts
2 cups chicken stock
½ teaspoon thyme
¼ teaspoon sage
¼ cup finely grated orange rind
   salt and pepper to taste

Grand Marnier-Currant Sauce:
1 (10 ounce) jar currant jelly
2 tablespoons Grand Marnier
2 tablespoons lemon juice
2 tablespoons pan juices from game hens

Saffron Chicken

2-3 **pounds chicken or 6 chicken thighs**
3½ **tablespoons olive oil**
salt and freshly ground black pepper to taste
1 **small onion, finely chopped**
1 **clove garlic, minced**
3½ **teaspoons paprika**
8 **fresh tomatoes, peeled, cored, seeded and finely chopped**
1½ **cups long grain white rice**
2½ **cups boiling water**
1 **large pinch of saffron strands, or ¼ teaspoon ground saffron**
1 **cup fresh broccoli flowerets**
4 **tablespoons fresh parsley**

1. Cut the chicken into serving pieces. Remove the skin. Heat the oil in a large skillet and fry the chicken, turning frequently to brown evenly. Season with salt and pepper, remove from pan, and set aside.

2. Add the onions and garlic to the juices in the sauté pan and cook slowly until softened but not colored. Add the paprika to the onions and fry quickly for about a minute to just <u>burn</u>. Add tomatoes to the sauté pan with the paprika and the onions. Cook for 5 to 10 minutes to reduce the liquid from the tomatoes. Stir the rice, water and saffron into the tomato puree. Add the browned chicken. Bring to a boil, reduce heat to simmering, cover tightly and cook for about 20 minutes.

3. Add the broccoli and parsley to the casserole, stir well and continue cooking for 5 to 10 minutes, or until the rice is tender and all of the liquid has been absorbed. Serve very hot. Yield: 6 servings.

Chicken Satay

1. Mix marinade ingredients and test for salt and sweetness. Pour over the chicken and marinate for 10 minutes to 1 hour.

2. Grill the chicken on a griddle or comal until cooked and browned.

3. To make Thai Peanut Sauce, heat the oil in a pot. Add curry paste and cook for 3 minutes. Add coconut milk, and water and boil for 5 to 10 minutes. Add sugar, salt and peanut butter. Test for salt and sweetness. Pour over the chicken. Serve with Jasmine rice or sautéed rice noodles. Yield: 4 to 6 servings.

The Thai Peanut Sauce is also an excellent salad dressing.

4-6 **chicken breasts**
Marinade:
½ **cup coconut milk**
1 **teaspoon sugar**
½ **teaspoon salt**
1 **tablespoon yellow curry powder**
2 **tablespoons oil**
Thai Peanut Sauce:
1 **tablespoon oil**
1 **teaspoon red curry paste, or to taste**
1 **cup coconut milk**
1 **cup water**
2 **teaspoons sugar**
½ **teaspoon salt**
½ **cup creamy peanut butter**

Red Curry Chicken

1. Poach chicken, bamboo shoots, bell pepper and basil quickly and set aside.

2. Heat the oil in a wok and add the curry paste. Cook for 2 minutes. Add the coconut milk and cook for 5 minutes. Add the stock, fish sauce and sugar. Immediately add the chicken and vegetable mixture. Taste for salt and sweetness. Serve with steamed rice. Yield: 3 to 4 servings.

Make no substitutions and leave nothing out because it changes the taste.

1 **cup sliced chicken**
½ **cup bamboo shoots, julienne cut**
½ **cup sliced bell pepper**
½ **cup fresh sweet basil**
1 **tablespoon oil**
1 **teaspoon red curry paste**
1 **cup coconut milk**
1 **cup chicken stock**
½ **tablespoon fish sauce**
½ **teaspoon sugar**

Chicken Marengo

6 **boneless chicken breasts, skinless**
¼ **cup butter**
1 **small onion, finely chopped**
1 **clove garlic, minced**
3 **tablespoons snipped fresh parsley**
1 **teaspoon salt**
1 **cup white wine**
2 **(8 ounce) cans tomato sauce**
¼ **pound fresh mushrooms, sliced**

1. Flour chicken and brown in butter or margarine. Add remaining ingredients, except mushrooms, blend and cover tightly. Place in a casserole and bake at 250 degrees for at least 2 hours. If sauce thickens too quickly during cooking, add more water or wine as needed.

2. Add mushrooms 5 minutes before serving. Serve with white rice. Yield: 6 servings.

A great party recipe, easily adapted to serve large numbers.

Lemon and Artichoke Chicken

1. Brown chicken in saucepan. Add garlic, lemon juice, white wine, chicken broth, salt and pepper. Cover and cook 25 minutes or until done.

2. Add capers and drained artichoke hearts, and heat through. Serve with buttered noodles or rice. Yield: 4 to 8 servings.

4   chicken thighs, skinless
4   chicken breast halves, skinless
4   tablespoons butter or margarine, and a little oil
2   cloves garlic, minced
1   lemon, juice only
⅓   cup white wine
½   cup chicken broth
    salt and pepper to taste
2   tablespoons capers, drained
1   (8½ ounce) can artichokes, halved

Lemon Chicken

1. Melt butter or margarine and mix with lemon juice. Stir in spices. Set aside.

2. Place chicken breasts in a 9x13 inch baking pan. Baste with the Lemon Sauce.

3. Bake at 350 degrees for 30 minutes or until done, basting often. Serve with rice. Yield: 8 servings.

8   chicken breast halves, skinned
Lemon Sauce:
½   cup butter or margarine
3   tablespoons lemon juice
1   heaping tablespoon dried oregano
1   tablespoon lemon pepper seasoning

Breast of Chicken Au Cheese and Mushroom Wine Sauce

6 chicken breast halves
1 cup bread crumbs
1 cup Parmesan cheese, divided
¼ teaspoon garlic powder
½ teaspoon salt
¼ teaspoon pepper
 pinch of oregano
 paprika
1 (10 ounce) can cream of mushroom soup
½ cup milk
¼ cup white wine
 parsley for garnish

1. Roll chicken in mixture of bread crumbs, ½ cup Parmesan cheese, garlic powder, salt, pepper, and oregano.

2. Place in a shallow baking pan in hot oven, 450 degrees, and cook for twenty minutes on each side.

3. Remove from oven and sprinkle with remaining ½ cup Parmesan cheese and paprika. Mix cream of mushroom soup, milk, and white wine. Pour over chicken and return to oven for another 20 minutes. Garnish with parsley and serve. Yield: 6 servings.

Buck Nibler

Chicken in Chablis Wine

4 large cloves fresh garlic, peeled
3 tablespoons butter
3 tablespoons olive oil
1 chicken (3 pounds), cut up
 salt and pepper to taste
2 cups California Chablis
1 (28 ounce) can whole peeled tomatoes, cut into quarters

1. Sauté garlic in butter and oil in large pan. Brown chicken. Season with salt and pepper. Cook until tender. Remove from pan and keep warm.

2. Scrape bits of chicken off pan while stirring in wine. Reduce sauce by half over high heat. Add tomatoes, stir well and cook over moderate heat for about 10 minutes.

3. Return chicken to pan, spooning sauce over chicken. Heat through and serve chicken in sauce. Yield: 4 servings.

Chicken Scaloppine with Hazelnuts

1. In a skillet, toast the hazelnuts on high heat, turning frequently. Remove from the pan. If unpeeled, squeeze most of their skin off with your finger tips (when you can handle them). While the hazelnuts are still warm, chop them into pieces no larger than rice kernels.

2. Put 3 tablespoons of the butter and all of the oil into the skillet, and turn the heat to high. Dredge the pounded chicken in flour on both sides and sauté. Do not crowd. Cook the scaloppine very briefly on both sides, to a light brown. Transfer to a platter and do the next batch.

3. Put the wine into the pan, scraping loose any cooking residue from the bottom. Add the hazelnuts. Simmer until the wine has evaporated completely. Stir in the remaining tablespoon of butter.

4. Sprinkle scaloppine with salt and pepper and return to pan. Include juice from the bottom of the platter. Turn 2 or 3 times.

5. Turn off heat. Pour the balsamic vinegar over the scaloppine. Turn them once or twice, then transfer to a warm serving dish with all of the pan juices. Serve at once. Yield: 6 servings.

1 **cup hazelnuts**
4 **tablespoons butter, divided**
1 **tablespoon vegetable oil**
6 **boneless chicken breasts, pounded very thin**
1 **cup flour**
⅔ **cup dry white wine**
salt and freshly ground pepper to taste
1 **tablespoon balsamic vinegar**

Chicken Pucci

½   cup olive oil
¼   cup chopped fresh
     parsley
1   clove garlic, minced
     juice of one lemon
3   whole chicken breasts,
     halved, boned,
     skinned, pounded
½   cup chopped pecans or
     walnuts
½   cup dark raisins
1   teaspoon salt
½   teaspoon pepper
1   cup flour
½   cup butter
6   fresh basil leaves or
     dried basil flakes
     salt and pepper to taste

1. Combine first 4 ingredients for marinade. Reserve ¼ cup. Marinate chicken breasts for a minimum of 2 hours.

2. Mix nuts, raisins and reserved ¼ cup of marinade together to make stuffing.

3. Put a spoonful of stuffing onto each breast and sprinkle with basil, roll up and skewer.

4. Mix salt and pepper with flour and dredge breasts in mixture.

5. Melt butter and brown chicken rolls, cooking 5 to 10 minutes.

6. Baste with remaining marinade and partially cover. Roast in 375 degree oven for 20 to 30 minutes. Yield: 6 servings.

This can be made ahead and reheated.

Chicken Breasts with Sun-Dried Tomatoes, Feta Cheese, Olives and Pine Nuts

1. Preheat oven to 350 degrees.

2. In large oven-proof skillet, cook onion in 1 tablespoon oil over moderate heat, stirring until softened. Add garlic and cook 1 minute.

3. Transfer mixture to a bowl and let cool. Stir in olives, pine nuts, tomatoes, cheeses and marjoram. Salt and pepper.

4. Insert sharp knife into thick end of each chicken breast and cut a lengthwise pocket. Fill each half breast with ¼ of the filling.

5. Clean skillet, heat remaining oil and brown the chicken. Transfer skillet to oven and bake for about 12 minutes. Yield: 4 servings.

½ cup finely chopped red onion
2 tablespoons olive oil, divided
1½ teaspoons minced garlic
½ cup green olives, cut into thin strips
¼ cup pine nuts, lightly toasted
½ cup drained, oil-packed sun-dried tomatoes, rinsed and cut into strips
¼ pound feta cheese, crumbled
2 tablespoons freshly grated Parmesan cheese
1 tablespoon fresh marjoram or 1 teaspoon dried
2 whole boneless chicken breasts, halved
salt and pepper to taste

Chicken Breasts in Phyllo

1½ **cups mayonnaise**
1 **cup chopped green onion**
⅓ **cup lemon juice**
2 **cloves garlic, minced**
2 **teaspoons dry tarragon**
12 **boneless, skinless chicken breast halves**
salt and pepper to taste
24 **sheets phyllo dough**
1⅓ **cups butter, melted**
⅓ **cup freshly grated Parmesan cheese**

1. Combine first 5 ingredients to make a sauce.

2. Lightly sprinkle chicken pieces with salt and pepper.

3. Place a sheet of phyllo on working surface. Quickly brush with butter (about 2 teaspoons). Place a second sheet on top of first. Brush with melted butter. Spread 1½ tablespoons of sauce on each side of chicken breast, (3 tablespoons in all). Place breast in one corner of buttered phyllo sheets. Fold corner over breast, then fold sides over and roll breast up in the sheets to form a package.

4. Place in an ungreased baking dish. Repeat with remaining breasts and phyllo sheets.

5. Brush packets with the rest of the butter and sprinkle with Parmesan cheese. At this point the dish may be tightly sealed and frozen. Thaw completely before baking. Bake at 375 degrees for 20 to 25 minutes, or until golden. Serve hot. Yield: 12 servings.

Grilled Chicken Breasts with Mango Avocado Salsa

1. Mix all ingredients except avocado and chicken in a large bowl, cover and chill. Can be prepared up to 3 hours ahead.

2. Add avocado to salsa and stir gently to combine. Season with salt and pepper.

3. Grill chicken. Top with salsa and serve. Yield: 4 servings.

You may add diced tomatoes, diced jícama and lime juice.

1   **large mango, peeled, pitted and diced**
3   **tablespoons minced onion**
3   **tablespoons diced green bell pepper**
3   **tablespoons diced red bell pepper**
1½ **tablespoons white wine vinegar**
1   **tablespoon chopped fresh cilantro**
1   **tablespoon olive oil**
1   **teaspoon minced fresh chives**
½   **large avocado, peeled, pitted and diced**
4   **boneless chicken breast halves**

*I can read a recipe;
Please, Mom, let me do it.
(I couldn't find the "scalded milk";
Bottom line: I blew it.)*

Roasted Garlic Chicken

1	whole large fryer
20	garlic cloves, divided
2	tablespoons butter or margarine, softened
½	teaspoon grated lemon peel
¼	teaspoon dry thyme
⅛	teaspoon dry rosemary
2	lemons, thinly sliced
	salt and pepper to taste

1. To loosen skin on chicken, start in at breast bone. Carefully work fingers under skin around breast and legs.

2. Peel and press 10 garlic cloves. Combine with butter, lemon peel, thyme and rosemary. Spread garlic butter under skin.

3. Place remaining garlic cloves and lemon slices into chicken body cavity. Season chicken lightly with salt and pepper.

4. Place on rack in roasting pan. Bake at 375 degrees for 1¼ to 1½ hours. When cooked, remove garlic cloves from cavity. Peel and serve with chicken or blend with butter and use as spread on thick slices of French bread. Yield: 6 to 8 servings.

Turkey Breakfast Sausage

1	pound ground turkey
¼	cup cold water
1½	teaspoons margarine
¼	teaspoon nutmeg
¼	teaspoon sage
1	teaspoon onion powder
1	teaspoon salt
½	teaspoon allspice
⅛	teaspoon cayenne pepper
¼	teaspoon poultry seasoning

1. Mix all ingredients, in order given, in mixing bowl. Turn onto chopping board, or other smooth surface, and shape into a 2½ inch roll about 7 inches long. Wrap in plastic wrap and refrigerate overnight. When ready to cook, remove from refrigerator and unwrap the roll. Slice meat into serving size pieces, approximately ½ inch thick.

2. Coat frying pan with nonstick cooking spray. Cook over low heat for 5 minutes on each side. Yield: 10 to 12 patties.

California Turkey Kabobs

1. Cut turkey into 1 inch cubes and place in plastic bag.

2. Combine picante sauce, oil, cumin, lemon juice, cayenne, and garlic. Mix well and pour into plastic bag with turkey and fasten securely. Place in refrigerator at least 4 hours or overnight, turning several times.

3. Drain turkey, saving marinade. Thread turkey and vegetables onto skewers. Place on grill over hot coals or on rack or broiler pan. Grill or broil until turkey is cooked through, turning and basting frequently with marinade. Serve with additional picante sauce. Yield: 4 to 5 servings.

2 pounds boneless turkey breast, or boneless, skinless chicken breast
1 cup picante sauce
⅛ cup vegetable oil
1 teaspoon ground cumin
1 teaspoon lemon juice
⅛ teaspoon cayenne pepper
1 clove garlic, minced
2 ears sweet corn, cut into 1 inch pieces
1 medium onion, cut into 6 wedges
1-2 sweet red peppers, cut into wedges
2 zucchini, cut into 1 inch pieces

Turkey-Almond Quiche

1 unbaked 9 inch pastry shell
1 (8 ounce) package cream cheese, softened
1¼ cups milk
2 large eggs
½ cup finely chopped toasted almonds
1¼ cups chopped turkey
¼ cup finely chopped green onion
1 chicken bouillon cube, crumbled
½ teaspoon salt
¼ teaspoon dry mustard
¼ teaspoon basil, crumbled
¼ teaspoon thyme
pepper to taste

1. Prepare pastry shell and set aside.

2. Beat cream cheese until smooth. Gradually beat in milk. Add eggs, one at a time, beating well after each addition. Set aside 1 tablespoon almonds. Stir remaining almonds, turkey, onion and seasoning into creamed mixture.

3. Pour into pastry shell and sprinkle reserved almonds over top. Bake below oven center at 375 degrees for 50 minutes or until knife inserted in center comes out clean. Yield: 4 to 6 servings.

California Turkey Treat

1. Melt margarine in large skillet. Add onion, green pepper, oregano and salt. Sauté until onion is transparent.

2. Add tomatoes and turkey. Simmer 5 minutes.

3. In a 2½ quart casserole, layer ½ the chips, Monterey Jack cheese and sauce. Repeat layer ending with sauce. Bake at 350 degrees for 20 to 25 minutes.

4. Spoon sour cream over top and sprinkle with shredded cheddar cheese. Bake an additional 5 to 8 minutes or until cheese melts. Garnish with chopped cilantro. Yield: 6 servings.

Chicken may be substituted for turkey.

4 tablespoons margarine
1 large onion, chopped
1 large green bell pepper, chopped
2 teaspoons oregano
1 teaspoon salt
1 teaspoon chili powder
1 (16 ounce) can tomatoes
1 (5½ ounce) package tortilla chips
pepper to taste
8 ounces Monterey Jack cheese, shredded
2 cups cooked turkey, cubed
1 cup sour cream
¼ cup cheddar cheese, shredded
cilantro for garnish

PRIZE WINNER • CALIFORNIA STRAWBERRY FESTIVAL

Tropic's Strawberry, Papaya and Mango Salsa

1 pint strawberries, hulled and diced into ¼ inch pieces

1 cup ¼ inch diced red papaya

1 cup ¼ inch diced ripe mango

1 (2 inch) fresh jalapeño pepper, seeded and chopped very fine

½ cup finely chopped red onions, soaked in ice water for 15 minutes, drained and patted dry

2 teaspoons balsamic vinegar (or more to taste)

¼ teaspoon salt

1. In a bowl, combine all ingredients and toss the mixture well. Serve the salsa with grilled poultry or seafood.

The salsa may be made 3 hours in advance and kept covered and chilled.

Wolfgang Hanau

Meat

GILROY GARLIC FESTIVAL
P. O. Box 2311
Gilroy, CA 95021
(408) 842-1625

The Gilroy Garlic Festival presents over 85 garlic foods with almost every ethnic background represented in the foods served. There are arts and crafts booths and four stages with live entertainment. Come eat until you can't hold anymore then wander through the arts and crafts area or enjoy the entertainment until you digest your food, then go eat some more! Takes place the last full weekend in July.

PATTERSON APRICOT FIESTA
P. O. Box 442
Patterson, CA 95363
(209) 892-3118

The Patterson Apricot Fiesta was launched in 1971 and is held in early June. The schedule of events includes a community dance, parade, public breakfast, queen pageant, "Little Miss and Mr. Apricot" contest, a crafts fair, firemen's muster, a petting zoo and the grand finale, a parachute jumping exhibition.

Individual Beef Wellingtons

1. Melt butter in frying pan over high heat and sear steaks on each side just to give brown color. Add wine. Swirl steaks in juice. Remove steaks and refrigerate.

2. Add shallots, mushrooms and garlic to frying pan. Cook over medium heat, stirring until all the liquid has evaporated. Chill the mushroom mixture.

3. Roll out pastry shells one at a time. On a lightly floured board make a circle 8 inches across. Put ⅙ of mushroom mixture in the center of the pastry. Place 1 steak on top. Sprinkle with salt and pepper. Fold pastry over steak and lay seam down on rimmed baking sheet. Repeat with rest of steaks. Cover and refrigerate as long as overnight. Take from refrigerator and bake in a 425 degree oven for 20 minutes or until pastry is light brown. While the Wellingtons are baking, prepare the Wine Sauce.

4. To prepare Wine Sauce, cook shallots, garlic and mushrooms in butter until mushrooms are barely cooked. Add wine and heat, stirring until liquid is reduced a little. Add salt and pepper to taste. Blend cornstarch with a little water to make a paste and add to the wine mixture, stirring until slightly thickened. Serve at once over Wellingtons. Meat will be rare. Yield: 6 servings.

6 small beef filet steaks cut 1 inch thick
1 tablespoon butter
6 tablespoons dry red or white wine
2 shallots, chopped fine
½ pound mushrooms, chopped fine
salt and pepper to taste
½ clove garlic, minced
1 package of 6 frozen patty shells, thawed

Wine Sauce:
2 tablespoons chopped shallots
½ clove garlic, minced
1 tablespoon butter
½-¾ pound mushrooms, sliced
½ cup dry red or white wine
salt and pepper to taste
1 tablespoon cornstarch

Marinated BB2 Steak

4-6 filets or 2 pounds London broil or 2 pounds sirloin steak

Marinade:
- ½ **cup soy sauce**
- 4 **tablespoons Worcestershire sauce**
- 1 **teaspoon hot pepper sauce**
  juice of one lemon
- ¼ **cup olive oil**
- 3-4 **garlic cloves, crushed**
- 2 **tablespoons bottled steak sauce**

1. Trim meat of unwanted fat.

2. Combine all of marinade ingredients in order given. Add steak to marinade coating both sides. Refrigerate, covered, for 24 hours. Turn meat 4 to 6 times in marinade during the 24 hours. One hour before cooking, allow meat to come to room temperature in the marinade. Prior to cooking, drain the meat from the marinade and pat dry. Cook over hot coals to desired doneness, basting with reserved marinade as desired. Yield: 4 to 6 servings.

Filet Mignon in Mushroom Sauce

- 1 **teaspoon butter**
- 1 **teaspoon peanut oil**
- 4 **(6 ounce) filets, 1½ inches thick**
- 1 **cup fresh mushrooms, sliced**
- 1 **tablespoon shallots or green onion, minced**
- ½ **cup dry white wine**
- ½ **cup stock**
- ¼ **cup ketchup**
- ½ **teaspoon cornstarch**
- 1 **teaspoon parsley, minced**

1. Sauté filets in butter and oil in hot frying pan to desired doneness. Remove from pan and keep warm.

2. Sauté mushrooms and shallots in same pan for 5 minutes. Add wine and deglaze pan. Add stock and ketchup mixed with cornstarch. Cook, stirring until slightly thickened and smooth. Pour sauce over meat and serve immediately. Yield: 4 servings.

Killer Filet of Beef

1. The day before serving, preheat oven to 425 degrees. Salt and pepper filet. In an oven-proof pan, melt 1 tablespoon butter and completely brown meat. Place in oven for 5 minutes. Pour consommé in the bottom of pan. Return to oven for 5 minutes more. Remove from oven. Cool meat at room temperature, basting occasionally. Refrigerate. When thoroughly chilled, remove from refrigerator and cut into ¼ inch slices.

2. In blender or food processor, blend ½ cup butter, parsley and garlic. Place 1 teaspoon of this mixture between each slice of meat and squeeze filet back together. Baste with consommé and return to refrigerator until the next day.

3. One hour before serving, remove from refrigerator. Preheat oven to 450 degrees. Place filet in oven for 7 minutes for medium rare or until cooked to desired doneness. Serve immediately. Yield: Varies.

1	large filet, any size
	salt and pepper to taste
1	tablespoon butter or oil
1	can consommé
½	cup butter
¾	bunch fresh parsley, long stems removed
2	cloves garlic, minced

Not the beaches, not the mountains,
Not the movies or the zoo;
America's favorite pastime
Is the backyard barbecue.

Italian Rump Roast

3-4	**pound rump roast**
3	**beef bouillon cubes**
1½	**cups water**
1	**tablespoon Italian seasoning**
1	**tablespoon instant minced onion**
1	**tablespoon parsley flakes**
1	**whole green pepper, diced**

1. Bake roast, uncovered, in 325 degree oven for 2 to 3 hours.

2. Mix beef bouillon cubes in water. Pour over beef. Sprinkle generously with Italian seasoning, instant minced onion, parsley flakes and diced green pepper. Cover roast and cook 2 hours longer. Cool and refrigerate. Allow roast to sit in juices overnight.

3. Remove from juices, slice thin and return to pan. Reheat prior to serving. Yield: 8 to 10 servings.

Sweet and Sour Short Ribs

5	**pounds short ribs, approximately 4 inches in length**
2	**cups sliced onions**
	flour
	salt and pepper

Sauce:

¾	**cup ketchup**
2	**tablespoons cider vinegar**
2	**tablespoons Worcestershire sauce**
4	**tablespoons soy sauce**
½	**cup sugar**
¾	**cup water**

1. Salt and pepper short ribs. Roll in flour. Arrange ribs in a 3 to 4 quart casserole and cover with onions separated into rings.

2. Combine sauce ingredients and pour over ribs, cover with foil and bake at 300 degrees for 3 hours. Yield: 8 servings.

Rosie's Terribly Spicy Ribs

1. In a glass or stainless steel bowl, combine marinade ingredients. Add ribs and turn to coat. Cover with plastic wrap and marinate in refrigerator for 24 hours or longer, turning occasionally.

2. Preheat oven to 325 degrees. Remove ribs from marinade and pat semi-dry. Combine coating mixture of garlic, ginger and sesame oil, and rub into meat. Combine ½ cup of sesame seeds with ½ cup of cilantro and roll ribs into this mixture. Bake for 20 minutes. Turn ribs, sprinkle with ½ the remaining cilantro and sesame seeds and bake for a further 20 minutes. Turn ribs, sprinkle with remaining cilantro and sesame seeds and bake for 15 minutes more or until tender. Yield: 4 servings as a main dish; 8 servings as an appetizer, cut into single rib pieces.

Rose Burtchby
Courtesy of the Gilroy Garlic Festival "Garlic Lovers Cookbooks."

1   rack (approximately 4 pounds) lean pork ribs, cut into double rib sections

Marinade:
3   cloves fresh garlic, crushed
1   teaspoon minced fresh ginger root
½   cup soy sauce
½   cup honey
½   cup dry sherry
½   cup vermouth

Coating:
5   tablespoons minced fresh garlic
3   tablespoons minced fresh ginger root
2   tablespoons Oriental sesame oil
1   cup sesame seeds, divided
1   cup finely chopped fresh cilantro, divided

Apricot Mushroom Beef Ribs

10 beef ribs
1 medium onion, sliced
1 tablespoon pickling spice
1 teaspoon salt

Sauce:
¼ pound diced mushrooms
1 cup diced apricots
2 tablespoons lemon juice
½ cup apricot wine
¾ cup ketchup
2 teaspoons prepared mustard
3 tablespoons light molasses
3 tablespoons Worcestershire sauce
3 teaspoons soy sauce
4 tablespoons vinegar
3 tablespoons brown sugar
2 tablespoons diced onion
dash of hot pepper sauce

1. Put beef ribs in pan and cover with water. (The ribs may be cut into smaller pieces if desired.) Add onion, pickling spice and salt. Heat slowly to a boil, lower heat and simmer for 1¼ hours. Remove from heat, cool in liquid.

2. For sauce, sauté mushrooms for 5 minutes. Place in blender with the remaining sauce ingredients. Mix well in blender.

3. Place sauce in pan and bring to a boil. (It is now ready to brush on ribs. This makes about 1½ pints of sauce which is enough for several helpings of ribs.)

4. When ready to broil ribs, remove from liquid and arrange in a single layer in a broiling pan. Brush with sauce and broil 4 inches from heat, turning after 5 minutes. Brush other side and broil another 5 minutes. Serve.

Iva Swift

Marinated Pork Tenderloin

1. Mix marinade ingredients. Pour over tenderloin. Marinate for 2 to 4 hours in refrigerator. Discard marinade.

2. Roast tenderloin in a 325 degree oven for approximately 30 to 40 minutes until meat thermometer registers 160 degrees.

3. To serve, slice on platter and garnish with sliced green onions. Yield: 5 to 6 servings.

Marinate as above, omitting sugar from marinade. Remove meat from marinade and pat dry. Coat with a mixture of ¼ cup honey and 2 tablespoons brown sugar then roll in white sesame seeds to cover. Roast in greased pan.

1 (1½ pound) pork tenderloin
   sliced green onions for garnish

Marinade:
½ cup soy sauce
½ cup dry red wine
½ teaspoon ground ginger
½ teaspoon dry mustard
1 clove garlic, minced
1 tablespoon sugar

Roast Pork Tenderloin

2 **boneless pork tenderloins, 1½ to 1¾ pounds each**
2 **tablespoons olive oil salt and pepper**
2 **sprigs fresh rosemary**
½ **cup red wine**
2 **tablespoons butter**
1 **onion, thinly sliced**
1 **orange, juice only**

1. Place 2 pork tenderloins in heavy roasting pan with 2 tablespoons oil. Roll meat in oil to coat, season with salt and pepper. Top with 2 sprigs of fresh rosemary.

2. Pour ¼ cup wine in pan and bake at 350 degrees for 15 minutes. Add more wine and bake 10 minutes longer. Remove meat to serving dish and cover with foil to keep warm.

3. Add butter to pan and quickly sauté onions. Add juice from orange. Cook over moderate-high heat for 5 minutes. Slice meat thinly and pour sauce over it.

4. Be sure not to overcook pork. Meat should be medium-rare when taken off heat, as it will continue to cook. Yield: 6 to 8 servings.

A young man was asked to a roast;
They asked him to please bring
* a toast.*
He thought they meant bread,
And found out instead
The toast was a roast for the host.

Pork Tenderloin with Sautéed Escarole

1. Sauté onions and garlic in 2 tablespoons of the olive oil until golden, not browned. Add escarole and sauté until wilted, but still a little crunchy. Remove to oven-proof serving platter and keep warm in very low oven.

2. Dredge pork slices in flour seasoned with salt and pepper. In same frying pan, add the remaining olive oil and sauté pork slices until browned. Arrange on top of escarole in serving dish.

3. Deglaze pan by adding butter and cooking over medium-high heat, scrape up browned bits of meat. Add wine and bring to a boil, then add orange juice and simmer for 5 minutes. Pour over meat and escarole, garnish with orange slices and serve immediately. Yield: 6 to 8 servings.

1 onion, chopped
2 cloves garlic, minced
1 large head escarole, chopped (or Swiss chard)
½ cup olive oil
2 boneless pork tenderloins (1½ to 1¾ pounds each), sliced ¼ inch thick
flour, seasoned with salt and pepper
2-4 tablespoons butter
½ cup Marsala wine
1½ cups orange juice
orange slices for garnish

Braised Pork Chops with Tomato and Garlic Sauce

4	tablespoons vegetable oil, divided
6	loin pork chops, ½ to 1 inch thick
1	teaspoon minced garlic
½	teaspoon oregano leaves, crumbled
¼	teaspoon thyme, crumbled
½	bay leaf
½	teaspoon salt
½	cup dry red wine
1	cup canned tomatoes, drained and very finely chopped
1	tablespoon tomato paste
½	pound green peppers, seeded and cut in 2x¼ inch strips (1½ cups)
½	pound mushrooms, sliced
	fresh chopped parsley (for garnish)

1. Heat 2 tablespoons oil in a heavy skillet. Brown chops for 2 to 3 minutes on each side and transfer to a plate. In remaining oil, cook garlic, oregano, thyme, bay leaf and salt for 30 seconds, stirring constantly. Spoon off excess oil, if any. Add wine and bring to a boil, stir in tomatoes and tomato paste and return chops to skillet. Cover and simmer over low heat until tender, 30 to 45 minutes, basting frequently.

2. In another skillet, heat remaining 2 tablespoons oil and fry green peppers for about 5 minutes, stirring frequently. Add mushrooms and cook for another minute, stirring frequently. Transfer to pan with pork chops. Cover and simmer for 5 minutes, uncover and cook for 10 more minutes or until sauce is medium-thick consistency.

3. To serve, arrange chops on heated platter and spoon vegetables and sauce over them. Garnish with fresh chopped parsley. Yield: 6 servings.

Pork Chops Milano

1. Trim chops and pound between waxed paper to ³⁄₁₆ inch thickness. Combine flour, salt and pepper, Parmesan cheese and parsley in shallow dish. Beat eggs in another shallow dish. Dip each chop into egg first, then flour and cheese mixture and place in single layer on waxed paper.

2. Preheat oven to 200 degrees. Pour oil in skillet to depth of ¼ inch. Place over medium-high heat and cook chops on both sides, 40 to 60 seconds per side. Drain on paper towel and keep warm in oven. (Or bake on greased baking sheet at 425 degrees for 5 to 8 minutes per side until golden brown.)

3. Discard oil and add butter and lemon peel and cook until golden brown. Stir in lemon juice and salt and pepper. Pour over chops and serve immediately. Yield: 4 servings.

4 **thin-cut pork chops**
½ **cup flour**
   salt and pepper
¼ **cup grated Parmesan cheese**
3 **tablespoons minced parsley**
2 **eggs**
   vegetable oil
4 **teaspoons unsalted butter**
   grated peel of ½ lemon
   juice of ½ lemon
   salt and pepper

Individual Lamb Roasts

1	**clove garlic**
2	**lamb shanks**
¼	**cup flour**
	salt
1	**teaspoon paprika**
2	**tablespoons vegetable oil**
¼	**cup lemon juice**
4	**peppercorns**
2	**bay leaves**
1	**large sweet potato, peeled and quartered**
½	**pound fresh small green beans**

1. About 2½ hours before dinner insert piece of garlic into each lamb shank. Combine flour, salt and paprika. Use to coat shanks.

2. In skillet, brown shanks on all sides. Place in 2 quart casserole. Add lemon juice to oil in skillet and stir to loosen brown bits. Pour over shanks. Add bay leaves and peppercorns. Cover shanks and bake 1 hour. Top with sweet potatoes and green beans. Sprinkle with salt. Cover and bake 1 hour longer or until meat and vegetables are tender. Yield: 2 servings.

Marinated Grilled Lamb Chops

8-10	**lamb chops, well trimmed**
	Marinade:
½	**cup dry sherry**
¼	**cup vegetable oil**
1	**medium onion, finely chopped**
2	**teaspoons Worcestershire sauce**
1	**tablespoon dry mustard**
½-1	**teaspoon dried rosemary**
½	**teaspoon thyme**
½	**teaspoon marjoram**
½	**teaspoon garlic salt**
½	**teaspoon freshly ground black pepper**

1. Mix marinade ingredients. Pour over lamb chops and marinate several hours.

2. Grill or barbecue lamb chops basting with marinade. Don't overcook. Yield: 4 to 5 servings.

Marinade can also be used for beef, veal or chicken. Add oregano or adjust herbs for other meats.

168

Veal with Lyonnaise Sauce

1. Sprinkle veal on both sides with salt, pepper and cayenne. Dredge well in flour, coating both sides. Heat butter and olive oil in a skillet over medium-high heat until bubbling. Shake scallops to remove excess flour and sauté 3 to 4 minutes on each side. Remove veal and set aside.

2. Add the wine and tomato paste to the skillet; deglaze the pan and dissolve tomato paste. Add the garlic and onion; cover and sauté until onions are tender. Stir in parsley. Return veal to pan and turn to coat in sauce. Serve on a platter with buttered noodles or steamed rice. Yield: 4 servings.

Brad Wallace, Dry Creek Vineyard

1   pound veal scallops, pounded thin
    salt, pepper and cayenne pepper to taste
    flour
½   cup butter
2   tablespoons olive oil
2   cloves garlic, minced
1   large yellow onion, minced
¾   cup dry white wine
2   tablespoons tomato paste
½   cup parsley, chopped

There once was a stir-fry gourmet;
His ribbons were all on display;
He dazzled his neighbors
With fruits of his labors –
A "cock of the wok", so they say.

Gilroy Green Card Casserole

3 ears fresh corn
10 whole tomatillos
2 jalapeño peppers
½ bunch fresh cilantro
10 cloves garlic, minced
1 teaspoon salt
½ teaspoon black pepper
6 pork chops, 1 inch thick
  corn chips
⅓ cup sour cream
½ teaspoon processed garlic puree

1. Peel husks from corn and tomatillos. Also remove corn silk. Cut whole corn kernels from ear and blanch in boiling, salted water until soft. Chop tomatillos; set aside. Remove seeds and dice jalapeño peppers. Chop cilantro. Mix corn, chopped tomatillos, jalapeños, chopped cilantro, minced garlic, salt and pepper together. Set aside.

2. Preheat oven to 350 degrees. Spray 2 quart casserole with nonstick spray. Place ½ the vegetable mixture in bottom of casserole. Place pork chops in a single layer over mixture and top with remaining vegetable mixture. Place uncovered casserole in preheated oven and bake for 1 hour. Remove from oven. Insert corn chips around the outside border of casserole dish. Combine sour cream and garlic puree. Serve with casserole. Yield: 6 servings.

**Debbie Sheesley
Courtesy of the Gilroy Garlic
Festival "Garlic Lovers
Cookbooks."**

170

Danish Meat Loaf

1. Mix pork with salt and pepper, water, egg, onion and potatoes. Chop 4 slices of bacon into small pieces and add to mixture. Shape into loaf and bake at 400 degrees for 10 minutes. Reduce heat to 350 degrees. Add rest of bacon over top. Bake 1 hour.

2. Add cream and cranberry jelly to the pan juices, if desired. Yield: 4 servings.

May substitute equal amount of ground turkey for ground pork.

1½	**pounds lean ground pork**
8	**slices bacon, divided**
2	**teaspoons salt**
1	**teaspoon pepper**
1	**cup water**
1	**egg**
1	**medium onion, grated**
3	**medium potatoes, grated**
½	**cup cream**
1	**tablespoon cranberry jelly**

Cannon Balls

1. Brown meat, onions, garlic and mushrooms. Stir in cheese, salsa and seasonings. Set aside.

2. Open rolls and take out some of the bread filling and mix with meat mixture. Toss. Stuff meat filling into rolls and close. Wrap individually in foil.

3. Bake at 350 degrees for about 30 minutes or until completely warm through. Yield: 6 to 8 servings.

Can also be frozen and heated at a later time.

1½	**pounds ground beef**
½	**onion, chopped**
1	**clove garlic, minced**
1	**pound fresh mushrooms, sliced**
1½	**pounds cheddar cheese, shredded**
2	**(6 ounce) cans salsa**
½	**teaspoon cumin**
	salt and pepper to taste
1	**bay leaf**
	dash of chili powder
6	**round sourdough rolls or 8 dinner rolls**

Tamale Pie

- 1 small onion, diced
- ½ green pepper, diced
- ½ cup chopped celery
- 1 tablespoon oil
- ½ pound lean ground beef
- 1 teaspoon salt, or to taste
- 1½ teaspoons chili powder
- 1½ teaspoons Worcestershire sauce
- 1 cup canned whole kernel corn
- 1¾ cups canned tomatoes
- ¼ cup cornmeal
- ½ cup sliced olives
- ½ cup cheddar cheese, shredded

This is a Wierd way to cook the cornmeal. use coarse cornmeal next x.

1. Brown onions, green peppers and celery in oil. Add meat and cook until brown. In a separate saucepan mix cornmeal with tomatoes. Cook for 5 to 10 minutes. Add to meat mixture. Stir in corn, seasonings and olives.

2. Pour into buttered casserole and top with cheese. Bake in 350 degree oven for 45 minutes. Can be prepared the day before and refrigerated. Yield: 3 to 4 generous servings.

Casserole freezes well before baking.

Remember that fellow, Jack Sprat,
The one who avoided all fat?
It was so long ago,
Did Mother Goose know
The nutritional value of that?

Ham Loaf with Zipper Sauce

1. Mix meats, cracker crumbs, onion, eggs, salt, milk and parsley until well blended. Shape into two 9x5x3 inch loaves. Bake in 350 degree oven for 30 minutes.

2. In a saucepan combine glaze ingredients and boil for 1 minute. Remove loaves from oven and baste with ½ of glaze mixture. Return to oven and bake for 1 hour, basting with remaining glaze after 30 minutes.

3. At this point the loaves may be frozen for later use. To serve cold, remove from freezer 1½ hours before meal. To reheat, thaw and bake at 325 degrees for 20 minutes. Mix Zipper Sauce ingredients. Serve. Yield: Each loaf serves 8 people.

2 **pounds lean ground smoked ham**
2 **pounds lean ground fresh pork**
1½ **cups cracker crumbs**
1½ **cups chopped onion**
4 **eggs, well beaten**
1¼ **teaspoons salt**
2 **cups milk**
2 **tablespoons chopped parsley**

Glaze:
½ **pound brown sugar**
½ **cup cider vinegar**
1½ **tablespoons dry mustard**

Zipper Sauce:
½ **cup mayonnaise**
½ **cup sour cream**
¼ **cup prepared mustard**
1 **tablespoon minced chives**
2 **tablespoons prepared horseradish**
salt, to taste
lemon juice, to taste

Swiss Ham Scalloped Potatoes

1½ cups Swiss cheese,
  shredded, divided
½ cup sliced green
  onions, including tops
1 tablespoon dill weed
2 tablespoons butter
2 tablespoons flour
1 teaspoon salt
1 cup milk
1 cup sour cream
6-7 cups thinly sliced
  potatoes
3 cups cooked ham,
  diced
¼ cup fine dry bread
  crumbs
¼ cup melted butter

1. In a small bowl toss together 1 cup Swiss cheese, onions and dill weed. Set aside.

2. Melt butter in a 1 quart saucepan, stir in flour and salt. Remove from heat, gradually stir in milk. Cook over medium heat, stirring constantly until thickened. Cook an additional 2 minutes. Remove from heat and stir in sour cream.

3. In a 3 quart buttered shallow baking dish, layer ⅓ of the potatoes, ½ of the ham, ½ of the cheese mixture and ½ of the sour cream mixture. Repeat, making the top layer with the last ⅓ of the potatoes. Combine the remaining ½ cup Swiss cheese, bread crumbs and melted butter. Sprinkle over the top of the casserole. Bake at 350 degrees for 30 to 35 minutes. Yield: 10 to 12 servings.

California Favorite Marinade

1 tablespoon lime juice
3 tablespoons olive oil
¼ teaspoon dry mustard
⅛ teaspoon thyme
⅛ teaspoon garlic salt
⅛ teaspoon cayenne
  pepper
½ teaspoon salt
⅛ teaspoon black pepper

1. Mix marinade ingredients well. Place meat and marinade in a shallow pan for 1 hour or overnight.

2. Remove and broil, bake or grill to desired doneness. Yield: 4 servings.

Great for flank steak or chicken breasts.

Vegetables

Castroville Artichoke Festival

CASTROVILLE ARTICHOKE FESTIVAL
Castroville, CA 95012
(408) 633-2465

Set in the self proclaimed "Artichoke Capitol of the World," the **Castroville Artichoke Festival** is one of the oldest agricultural festivals in California. The Festival is a two-day affair in September which includes a parade with floats and marching bands, a firemen's muster, a 10K run, a queen contest (the first Artichoke Queen was Marilyn Monroe), food booths, and a recipe contest.

DEL MAR FAIR
2260 Jimmy Durante Blvd.
Del Mar, CA 92014
(619) 755-1161

The Del Mar Fair is San Diego County's annual Agricultural Association fair and attracts more than a million guests each summer. The Del Mar Fair consistently ranks as the second largest fair in California, and one of the nation's top fairs in attendance. Since its inception in the late 1880's, the county fair has emphasized education and entertainment. There is also lots of family-oriented fun at the Del Mar Fair —educational agriculture exhibits, livestock barns, a gorgeous flower and garden show, thrilling rides, top-name entertainment, and games, contests and food galore! Runs mid June through July 4th.

Stuffed Artichokes

1. Soak artichokes in lemon water.

2. Whack artichokes face-down on countertop to open them up.

3. Prepare stuffing by mixing bread crumbs with the Parmesan cheese, oregano or mint, salt and pepper.

4. Drizzle the inside of the artichokes with olive oil, opening the leaves to be sure all of them have some of the bread mixture.

5. Drizzle top with olive oil.

6. Place artichokes on rack in large covered pan, with 1½ to 2 inches of water. Simmer for 1 hour or until tender, adding water as needed.

7. Cool and serve at room temperature. Yield: 8 servings.

4　**large artichokes, cleaned with top ⅓ cut off and bottom leaves removed**
2　**cups dried bread crumbs**
½　**cup grated Parmesan cheese**
½　**cup oregano or fresh mint, chopped**
　salt and pepper to taste
　olive oil

Spinach Artichoke Casserole

1. Place artichokes in greased 1½ quart baking dish. Spread spinach over artichokes.

2. Blend cream cheese with butter, then mix in milk, salt and pepper.

3. Spread cheese mixture over spinach. Top with Parmesan cheese. Cover and bake at 350 degrees for 30 minutes. Uncover and bake for 10 minutes more. Yield: 8 servings.

2　**(6 ounce) jars marinated artichokes, drained**
1　**(20 ounce) package chopped spinach, thawed and drained**
1　**(8 ounce) package cream cheese, softened**
2　**tablespoons butter**
4　**tablespoons milk**
　salt and pepper to taste
½　**cup grated Parmesan cheese**

Thistle Pie

4 **medium artichokes**
  juice of ½ lemon
¼ **cup olive oil**
2 **carrots, cut into match
  sticks**
½ **onion, minced**
1 **clove garlic, minced**
2 **tablespoons chopped
  parsley**
½ **teaspoon salt
  freshly ground black
  pepper, to taste**
¾ **cup ricotta**
½ **cup freshly ground
  Parmesan cheese**
2 **eggs**

1. Trim artichokes by snapping off leaves (snap off all the hard outer leaves), exposing the tender heart. Trim away all the dark green tops and remaining leaves. Do not detach stem, but peel away the green rind all the way down to the tender core. Cut the artichoke in half, remove the choke and prickly inner leaves. Then slice them as thin as you can, lengthwise. Put them in a bowl with enough water to cover and the juice of ½ lemon.

2. Sauté onions, carrots and parsley in olive oil until onions are light gold.

3. Drain and rinse artichokes. Sauté with onions and carrots for 1 minute. Add garlic, salt and pepper to taste. Add ½ cup water. Cook until tender, 7 to 15 minutes on low heat, add more water if needed. Allow to cool. Add the ricotta and Parmesan cheeses. Beat eggs, and add to mixture.

4. Preheat oven to 375 degrees. Mix flour, butter, ricotta and salt in a bowl, using a fork or pastry cutter. Turn out onto a work surface. Knead for 5 minutes until smooth. Divide the dough into two parts, one twice as big as the other. Roll out the larger piece to ⅓ inch thickness on kitchen parchment paper sprinkled with grated Parmesan cheese. Place in greased and floured 8 inch spring-form pan, covering the bottom and letting it come up the sides. Smooth out any thick folds with your fingers. Pour in filling and smooth with a spatula. Roll remaining dough on kitchen parchment and slip over pie, covering completely. Trim any excess leaving ½ inch, pinch edges together. Place in upper level of oven for 45 minutes until brown on top.

5. Unmold and serve lukewarm or at room temperature. Yield: 6 to 8 servings.

Noel Kelsch

Pastry:
- 1½ **cups flour**
- ½ **cup butter, softened to room temperature**
- ¾ **cup ricotta**
- ½ **teaspoon salt**

The veggies were having a picnic;
Some of the guests missed the food;
The beets and the onions got pickled;
The prunes and tomatoes got stewed.

Portuguese Beans

1	**pound pink beans**
1	**pound hamburger**
1	**large yellow onion**
1-2	**large cloves garlic**
½-1	**pound ham hock or leftover ham**
1	**(4 ounce) can diced green chiles**
1	**(28 ounce) can whole tomatoes**
1-2	**teaspoons ground cumin**
1	**teaspoon seasoned salt**
1	**teaspoon salt, or to taste**
	pepper
2	**bay leaves**
	chili powder, to taste (optional)

1. Rinse and soak beans overnight; or, rinse, cover with 2 quarts water and boil quickly for 2 minutes. Turn off heat and soak, covered, for 1 hour. Pour off soaking water. Cook beans very slowly in water, just to cover, with 2 teaspoons salt for 1½ to 2 hours until tender, but not falling apart.

2. Fry hamburger meat, pour off excess fat, add chopped onions and garlic, and sauté with hamburger until limp. Add ham, chiles, tomatoes (broken up with juice) and spices. Simmer for 15 to 30 minutes. When beans are tender, pour off cooking liquid. Liquid may be reserved and used later in soup, if desired.

3. Pour tomato sauce mixture over the beans, adjust salt and pepper, and simmer for additional ½ hour. Serve. Yield: 2½ quarts or 20 one-half cup servings.

To make this ahead of time, skip the additional cooking time, and plan on reheating very slowly for about 1 hour, being careful to avoid burning. Freezes very well, or can be kept in the refrigerator for about 1 week.

Bean and Rice Loaf

1. Soak the beans overnight, drain. Cover with water, add the onion, garlic and salt and cook until tender. Drain. Place in a large bowl and mash. Leave some beans whole for texture. Add the cooked rice.

2. Sauté the vegetables in oil until tender and add to the bean mixture. Stir in the bread crumbs, tomato sauce and spices.

3. Butter a 9x5x3 inch loaf pan and sprinkle sesame seeds over the bottom. Add bean and rice mixture. Bake at 375 degrees for 20 minutes uncovered. Sprinkle with cheese and bake an additional 10 minutes. Yield: 8 to 10 servings.

1	cup dried pinto beans
1	cup dried kidney beans
1	medium onion
3	garlic cloves
1	teaspoon salt
1	cup brown rice, cooked
1	tablespoon oil
1	cup chopped celery
1	cup chopped onion
½	cup chopped green pepper
2	garlic cloves, minced
1	cup seasoned bread crumbs
1¼	cups tomato sauce
1	teaspoon dried basil
½	teaspoon chili powder
½	teaspoon cumin
2	tablespoons dried parsley
	salt and pepper to taste
2	tablespoons sesame seeds
½	cup shredded cheddar cheese

Blue Cheese Broccoli

1. Barely cook broccoli. Drain.

2. Place in a 7x11 inch or comparable baking dish.

3. Mix blue cheese into white sauce. Pour on top of broccoli. Bake at 325 degrees for 30 to 45 minutes. Great with any beef dish. Yield: 6 to 8 servings.

2	(10 ounce) packages frozen broccoli
2	cups medium white sauce
2-4	ounces blue cheese

Cannellini Beans with Cooked Greens

2   (15 ounce) cans
    cannellini beans
3   cloves garlic, minced
1   sprig rosemary
    salt and pepper to taste
1   bunch escarole or
    Swiss chard
1   small onion or 2
    shallots, minced
3   tablespoons balsamic
    vinegar
¼   cup olive oil
    freshly ground black
    pepper, to taste

1. Sauté 2 cloves garlic and rosemary in small pan for 4 to 5 minutes (don't brown garlic). Add beans (including juice) and salt if necessary. Cook together for 5 to 10 minutes; let sit.

2. Put remaining clove garlic and onions or shallots in large sauté pan with vinegar and oil. Add greens and cook quickly over medium heat until wilted.

3. Add bean mixture to pan, heat through and season to taste, adding more oil or vinegar as needed. Yield: 6 servings.

Caponata

1   large red onion, sliced
1   cup celery, diced
    olive oil
2   medium eggplants,
    cubed
1   (7 ounce) can tomato
    sauce
¼   cup vinegar (balsamic,
    preferably)
3   tablespoons sugar
3-4 tablespoons capers
1   (2½ ounce) can
    chopped olives
    fresh basil, chopped

1. Sauté onion and celery in olive oil 10 to 15 minutes, set aside.

2. Sauté eggplant in oil, stirring often, adding oil as needed until eggplant is tender and lightly browned, 20 to 25 minutes.

3. Combine tomatoes, vinegar, sugar, capers and olives and stir into egg-plant. Add onion and celery. Simmer on low heat for 20 to 30 minutes, stirring often. Garnish with basil and serve at room temperature with sliced baguettes or focaccia. Yield: 6 to 8 servings.

This recipe freezes well.

Place caponata in shallow baking dish and dot with slices of goat cheese. Bake for 10 minutes at 350 degrees. Serve immediately.

Chile Relleno Casserole

1. Mix half-and-half, eggs and flour.

2. Alternate layers of egg mixture, chiles and cheeses in 8 inch square pan.

3. Bake at 350 degrees for 1 hour. Top with your favorite Mexican salsa and serve. Yield: 4 to 6 servings.

1 **cup half-and-half**
2 **eggs**
⅓ **cup flour**
1 **(4 ounce) can diced green chiles**
½ **pound Monterey Jack cheese, shredded**
½ **pound cheddar cheese, shredded**
   cumin, salt and pepper to taste

Mushroom Treat

1. Stem mushrooms so that you have nice caps.

2. In a 12 inch skillet, sauté caps in butter, adding spices. Serve Immediately. Yield: 6 to 8 servings.

1 **pound large mushrooms**
2 **tablespoons butter liberal sprinkling of nutmeg**
1 **pinch (each) curry, coriander, salt and lemon pepper**
1 **squeeze lemon juice**

Mushroom Casserole

1. Clean mushrooms and place in a 1 quart casserole. Melt butter and mix together with rest of ingredients. Pour over mushrooms. Bake in 350 degree oven for 20 minutes. Serve immediately. Yield: 4 servings.

1 **pound whole, small mushrooms**
½ **cup butter, melted**
1 **tablespoon chopped fresh marjoram or rosemary (½ teaspoon dried)**
1 **tablespoon minced chives**
½ **cup chicken bouillon**
½ **cup dry white wine**
1 **teaspoon salt freshly ground black pepper to taste**

Eggplant Parmigiana

1   small eggplant, sliced
    into 4 (¾ inch) rounds,
    ends cut off
2   tablespoons olive oil
2   cups Special Tomato
    Sauce, divided
1   teaspoon vegetable
    seasoning
½   teaspoon dried whole
    oregano
1   cup fresh sliced
    mushrooms
½   cup diced celery
½   cup diced bell pepper
3   tablespoons freshly
    grated Parmesan
    cheese
3   tablespoons chopped
    fresh parsley
12 slices mozzarella
    cheese (about 6
    ounces)

1. To prepare Special Tomato Sauce, gently sauté garlic and shallots in oil. Add basil, bay leaf, tomatoes and pepper. Cover and simmer for 5 minutes. Simmer uncovered for an additional 10 to 15 minutes. Add tomato puree and water. Simmer uncovered for 20 minutes until sauce has thickened. Sprinkle with parsley and cheese and mix.

2. Brush both sides of eggplant with oil. Broil on both sides until lightly browned, but not cooked. Place 1 cup of Special Tomato Sauce in baking dish just large enough to hold eggplant slices. Set slices on top of sauce. Sprinkle with vegetable seasoning and oregano.

3. Preheat oven to 350 degrees.

4. Heat remaining cup of Special Tomato Sauce with mushrooms, celery and bell pepper. Add grated cheese and parsley. Cover eggplant with sauce. Top each eggplant slice with 3 slices of mozzarella. Cover and bake at 350 degrees for 40 minutes. Serve immediately. Yield: 4 servings.

Special Tomato Sauce:
- 2 teaspoons olive oil
- 2 teaspoons minced garlic
- 4 teaspoons minced shallots
- 1 tablespoon dried sweet basil
- 1 bay leaf
- 1 (18 ounce) can whole plum tomatoes or 6 fresh tomatoes, peeled & diced
- 1 teaspoon freshly ground black pepper
- 1 cup tomato puree
- ¼ cup water
- 3 tablespoons chopped fresh parsley
- 2 tablespoons grated Parmesan cheese

There once was a young farmerette
Who grew all the corn she could get;
And so, year by year,
She played it by ear
To pay off her mortgage and debt.

Red Cabbage

1 **(3 pound) head of red cabbage**
3 **tablespoons butter**
1 **tablespoon sugar**
½ **cup vinegar**
½ **cup currant jelly**
1 **teaspoon salt (optional)**

1. Slice cabbage very fine into a large casserole with a lid. Melt butter, add to cabbage with sugar and vinegar. Mix well. Microwave or cook on low heat for 30 to 60 minutes, until tender. Add jelly and salt if desired, cook 10 minutes longer. Yield: 6 to 8 servings.

Potatoes Romanoff

6 **large potatoes**
2 **cups large-curd cottage cheese**
1 **cup sour cream**
1 **small clove garlic, minced**
1 **teaspoon salt**
2 **green onions, finely chopped**
1 **cup shredded cheddar cheese**
 paprika

1. Peel potatoes and boil until they are just tender (not soft). Cut into ¼ inch cubes and combine with the cottage cheese, sour cream, garlic, salt and green onions.

2. Turn into buttered casserole and top with grated cheese. Sprinkle with a small amount of paprika. Bake at 350 degrees for 30 minutes. Yield: 6 to 8 servings.

This recipe can be prepared ahead of time and refrigerated. Allow additional cooking time to heat through.

Potatoes Monterey

1. Melt butter in large skillet over medium heat, add potatoes and cook until browned and crisp.

2. Add cheese, tomatoes, and onions and stir until cheese melts. Season with salt. Gently mix in avocado. Spoon onto plates, top with sour cream and serve. Yield: 4 to 6 servings.

3 tablespoons butter
3 medium baking potatoes, unpeeled, boiled and diced
1½ cups shredded Monterey Jack cheese
1½ cups shredded cheddar cheese
⅔ cup diced tomatoes, peeled and seeded
2 tablespoons minced onion
2 tablespoons minced green onion
½ cup diced avocado
½ cup sour cream

Potato Surprise

1. Scrub potatoes and thinly cut round-wise. Place in a 7x9 inch glass baking dish upright (potato slices are not laid down).

2. Mix rest of ingredients in small bowl.

3. Brush ½ of mixture on potatoes, put in oven and bake 15 minutes. Remove from oven and brush on the rest of the mixture. Return to oven and bake another 15 minutes. Check potatoes to be sure they are done. Baking an additional few minutes may be necessary. Yield: 8 servings.

8 new potatoes
¼ cup vegetable oil
2 tablespoons Parmesan cheese
1 heaping tablespoon dried onion flakes
½ teaspoon salt
½ teaspoon white pepper
¼ teaspoon paprika

Potato Cheese Casserole

5   **medium potatoes,
      peeled and diced**
2   **teaspoons salt**
2   **tablespoons butter**
2   **eggs**
2   **tablespoons finely
      chopped chives or
      scallions**
¼   **cup finely chopped
      parsley**
1   **cup shredded
      mozzarella cheese**
2   **tablespoons grated
      Parmesan cheese
      white pepper**

1. Cover potatoes with water, add salt, and cook. Drain, reserving some of the cooking liquid. Mash the potatoes with the butter and a little of the cooking liquid. Beat eggs and mix into potatoes using an electric mixer.

2. Spread ⅓ of potato mixture on bottom of 1½ quart buttered casserole. Sprinkle with ½ of chives, parsley and mozzarella cheese. Repeat, then cover with remaining third of potatoes and sprinkle with Parmesan cheese. Bake, uncovered, in 350 degree oven for 45 minutes. Yield: 10 to 12 servings.

This is a good party dish as it can be made well in advance. It will keep in the refrigerator for 2 days, or it can be frozen before it is cooked. Allow to defrost in refrigerator before baking.

New Potatoes in Sour Cream

25-30   **small new potatoes**
1   **medium onion,
      chopped**
6   **tablespoons butter**
3   **cloves garlic, minced
      small bunch chives,
      minced
      parsley, snipped**
1   **cup sour cream
      salt and pepper to taste**

1. Boil new potatoes until tender. Drain.

2. Melt butter in skillet, add onions and garlic and sauté until translucent. Add potatoes and stir until mixed. Cook 4 to 5 minutes. Add sour cream, chives and parsley. Season to taste. Serve immediately. Yield: 4 to 6 servings.

If you can't find small new potatoes, cut larger ones after boiling.

Roquefort-Stuffed Potatoes

1. Preheat oven to 450 degrees.

2. Wash potatoes, dry and rub skins with a little salad oil. Bake until tender, about 45 minutes. Remove from oven and cut in half lengthwise. Scoop out pulp, being careful not to break the skins.

3. Mash potatoes well with electric mixer, beat in butter or margarine, milk and sour cream. Beat until mixture is light and fluffy. Crumble Roquefort cheese and stir into potato mixture, add the chives, salt and pepper.

4. Pile the mashed potatoes back into the shells, mounding them slightly. Return to oven for 8 to 10 minutes. Serve hot. Yield: 12 servings.

Potatoes can be prepared ahead of time and either refrigerated for 1 day or frozen for several months.

6 **medium-large baking potatoes**
4 **tablespoons margarine or butter**
3 **tablespoons milk**
1 **cup sour cream**
5 **tablespoons (3 ounces) Roquefort cheese**
2 **tablespoons minced chives**
salt to taste
freshly ground black pepper

Make-Ahead Potatoes

1. Cook peeled potatoes in salted boiling water until tender. Drain and mash. Add remaining ingredients and beat until light and fluffy.

2. Cool, cover and place in refrigerator. When ready to use place in greased casserole, dot with butter and bake about 30 minutes in a 350 degree oven. Yield: 8 to 12 servings.

5 **pounds potatoes**
2 **(3 ounce) packages cream cheese**
1 **cup sour cream**
1 **teaspoon salt**
½ **teaspoon pepper**
2 **tablespoons butter**

Sweet Potato and Banana Casserole

4	**medium sweet potatoes**
4	**tablespoons butter**
1½	**teaspoons salt**
4	**bananas, sliced**
¾	**cup brown sugar**
¾	**cup orange juice**

1. Cook potatoes until tender. Cool, peel and slice ¼ inch thick.

2. Layer potatoes and bananas, banana layer last. Dot potato layers with butter and salt. Sprinkle sugar over bananas. Add orange juice. Bake in 350 degree oven for 30 minutes. Yield: 6 to 8 servings.

Yams with Water Chestnuts

2	**(16 ounce) cans yams, drained**
1	**(9 ounce) can crushed pineapple**
2	**cooking apples, diced**
1	**(5 ounce) can water chestnuts, diced**
	salt and pepper to taste
3	**tablespoons butter or margarine**
⅓	**cup sugar**
	reserved pineapple juice
1	**jigger of rum**
½	**tablespoon cinnamon**
½	**tablespoon ground ginger**

1. Mash yams. Strain pineapple, reserving juice for syrup. Add pineapple, then apples, water chestnuts and salt, to potatoes.

2. Make syrup of butter, sugar, pineapple juice, rum and spices. Stir syrup into potato mixture. Place in buttered casserole and bake, uncovered, in 350 degree oven for 45 minutes. Yield: 9 to 12 servings.

Spinach and Onion Mold

1. Preheat oven to 350 degrees. Heat water to boiling in a large pan. Drop 8 to 10 romaine leaves in the water and leave just until wilted (about 1 minute). Remove, drain well, and arrange leaves, overlapping in greased 1½ quart baking mold. Line dish completely with romaine leaves.

2. Sauté onions in butter until soft; stir in flour, salt and dill and remove from heat. Slowly stir in milk and return to heat and cook over medium-high heat, stirring constantly until thickened.

3. Beat eggs in large bowl. Add hot onion sauce, beating well. Stir in spinach, cracker crumbs and cheese and spoon into prepared mold. Cover with foil.

4. Set mold in large pan, at least 3 inches deep. Pour boiling water into pan, halfway up sides of mold. Bake at 350 degrees for 1 hour or until center is almost set, remove from water.

5. To remove from mold, place serving plate over mold, invert and turn out. Garnish with tomato roses, lemon slices, green olive slices or halves. Serve warm or at room temperature. Yield: 8 to 10 servings.

1 large head romaine lettuce
3 (10 ounce) packages frozen chopped spinach, cooked, drained and squeezed dry
1 cup minced onion
6 tablespoons butter
¼ cup flour
1 teaspoon salt
¼ teaspoon dill weed
1½ cups milk
5 eggs
½ cup cracker crumbs
½ cup grated Parmesan cheese
tomato roses, lemon slices and/or green olive slices or halves as garnishes

Pasta Vegetable Pie

2 **cups all-purpose flour**
¾ **teaspoon salt, divided**
¾ **cup shortening**
2 **cups rotini pasta (1 cup spinach flavored and 1 cup plain)**
2 **medium red bell peppers, cut into 1 inch strips**
2 **medium yellow bell peppers, cut into 1 inch strips**
1 **medium onion, chopped**
2 **tablespoons olive oil**
1 **teaspoon dried basil**
¼ **teaspoon Italian seasoning**
¼ **teaspoon pepper**
1 **egg**
1 **(15 ounce) container part-skim ricotta cheese**
1 **(10 ounce) package frozen spinach, thawed and squeezed dry**
1 **cup shredded part-skim mozzarella cheese**
1 **cup marinara sauce**

1. In a bowl, mix flour and ¼ teaspoon salt. With pastry blender, cut in shortening until mixture resembles coarse crumbs. Stir 5 to 6 tablespoons very cold water into flour mixture until dough holds together. Shape into a ball and cover with plastic wrap.

2. Prepare pasta as label directs, but do not add salt to water. Drain.

3. In a 12 inch skillet, sauté onion in olive oil for 5 minutes. Add peppers, basil, Italian seasoning, pepper and ¼ teaspoon salt. Cook, stirring occasionally, until vegetables are tender.

4. In a cup, beat egg slightly. Reserve 1 tablespoon beaten egg. In a medium bowl, mix remaining egg with ricotta cheese, spinach and ¼ teaspoon salt.

5. Preheat oven to 400 degrees. Grease a 9 inch spring-form pan.

6. On slightly floured board, roll ⅔ of dough into a 15 inch round. Fit into pan, allowing dough to hang over side of pan slightly. Sprinkle bottom of crust with cheese, top with ½ of the sautéed pepper mixture. Spread ½ of the ricotta cheese mixture over pepper mixture. Add marinara sauce, then pasta. Top with remaining ricotta and pepper mixtures. Roll out remaining dough to 11 inch round. Lay dough over filling, allowing dough to hang over side of pan. Fold overhang toward center, pinching dough all

around to make a stand-up edge. Flute. Brush top of dough with remaining egg. Make pastry decorations for the top, brushing with a little bit of the egg. Make holes or slits to allow steam to escape during baking. Bake pie for 55 to 60 minutes. Yield: 8 servings.

Tulie Trejo

Stuffed Grape Leaves

1. Combine all ingredients except grape leaves.

2. Lay grape leaves flat and place a heaping teaspoonful of the mixture in the center.

3. Starting at the stem end, roll leaves away from you, tightly turning in the sides to prevent filling from coming out.

4. Arrange stuffed rolls in compact layers in a large saucepan. Place a heavy pottery dish on top of the rolls to prevent them from coming apart when boiling.

5. Add 1½ to 2 cups of hot water and bring to a boil over high heat. Reduce heat and cook over medium-low heat for 30 to 35 minutes.

6. Remove from heat and drain. Serve hot or cold, garnish with lemon wedges. Yield: 6 to 8 servings.

Can be made 1 or 2 days ahead and refrigerated.

¼ **cup butter, melted**
1 **cup canned tomatoes, broken into small pieces**
1 **medium onion, finely chopped**
½ **cup long grain rice, cooked**
2 **tablespoons parsley, finely chopped**
½ **teaspoon dried mint flakes, or 1 teaspoon dried dill**
½ **teaspoon salt**
⅛ **teaspoon pepper**
1 **(15 ounce) jar grape leaves (sold in specialty stores) lemon wedges for garnish**

Torta of Spinach and Crêpes

Crêpes:
- 2 **eggs**
- 1 **cup milk**
- ⅔ **cup flour**
- ¼ **teaspoon salt**
- 2 **tablespoons butter, melted**

Filling:
- 2 **cloves garlic, minced**
- 3 **tablespoons olive oil**
- 1 **cup tomato puree, or fresh tomatoes, peeled, seeded and cut up**
- 1 **(10 ounce) package spinach, drained well**
- ¼ **teaspoon salt**
- ½ **tablespoon butter**
- ½ **pound shredded ham, or cooked and crumbled Italian sausage**
- ½ **cup grated Parmesan cheese**
- 1 **cup shredded Monterey Jack cheese**

1. Place ingredients for crêpes in blender or food processor and process until smooth. Let stand, covered, for 1 hour.

2. Brush bottoms of two nonstick 8 or 9 inch fry pans with melted butter; heat both pans over medium heat. Pour scant ¼ cup batter onto one pan, tip to coat bottom. Cook 2 minutes until top looks dry and underside is just browned. Gently loosen crêpe with spatula and shake pan to loosen. Invert crêpe into empty skillet and cook for 30 seconds. Meanwhile, begin cooking another crêpe in first pan. Slip each cooked crêpe onto waxed paper. Stack crêpes on top of each other as they are cooked. Can be made ahead and frozen or refrigerated. Bring to room temperature before using.

3. Sauté garlic in oil in small saucepan until golden. Stir in tomatoes, parsley, salt and spinach. Simmer 5 to 10 minutes.

4. Butter a 9 inch pie plate with ½ tablespoon butter. Stack crêpes with light coating of sauce, meat and cheeses. Save some sauce for top, dot with butter and sprinkle with Parmesan cheese.

5. Bake at 400 degrees for 15 minutes. Cut into wedges to serve. Yield: 6 servings.

Great for picnics. Bake just before leaving, remove from oven and wrap in foil then newspapers for insulation.

Desserts

California Strawberry Festival

CALIFORNIA STRAWBERRY FESTIVAL
1621 Pacific Avenue #127
Oxnard, CA 93033
(805) 385-7578

The California Strawberry Festival provides "fruitful" fun for visitors of all ages on the third weekend in May. The city of Oxnard, which produces more than 20 percent of California's strawberries, rolls out the red carpet for more than 70,000 guests who indulge in gourmet strawberry foods, strawberry tart tossing and strawberry shortcake eating contests, a smorgasbord of live musical entertainment, a top-quality fine arts and crafts show featuring more than 200 booths, Strawberryland for children and more.

CHERRY FESTIVAL
P. O. Box 557
Linden, CA 95236
(209) 887-3767

The second weekend in May is the time for cherry treats and lots of fun in Linden. There is a parade, farmers' market, carnival rides, equipment show, car show, lots of children's games and a variety of entertainment and music.

Strawberries in Mascarpone Cream

1. Beat the egg yolks with the sugar and cornstarch until thick and lemon colored. Scald ½ cup of the cream with the vanilla bean. Cool slightly.

2. Gradually beat the scalded cream into the egg yolk mixture. Pour into a saucepan and cook over medium heat, stirring constantly, until the mixture just reaches the boiling point. Remove from heat immediately. Strain (to remove the vanilla bean) into a mixing bowl and set the bowl in a pan of cold water to cool. Stir often. When completely cool, beat in the mascarpone. Lightly whip the remaining cream and fold into the mascarpone mixture. Chill.

3. Clean the strawberries and halve lengthwise. About ½ hour before serving, sprinkle with all but 1 tablespoon of the sugar and the liqueur. Stir to coat evenly. Cover and reserve.

4. If using pine nuts, toast in a nonstick pan without fat. Divide the strawberries among 6 flat plates or shallow soup bowls. Top with the mascarpone cream. Sprinkle with the remaining brown sugar. Drizzle with liqueur and top with nuts. Yield: 8 servings.

Melody Favish

3   **egg yolks**
⅓   **cup sugar**
½   **teaspoon cornstarch**
1   **cup whipping cream**
½   **vanilla bean, split lengthwise**
1   **cup mascarpone cheese**
8   **cups perfectly ripe strawberries**
½   **cup light brown sugar (Demerara is best but hard to find)**
½   **cup almond-flavored liqueur**
½   **cup pistachios or pine nuts**

Hot Chocolate Soufflé with Cold Vanilla Sauce

2 **tablespoons butter, softened**
3 **tablespoons granulated sugar**
3 **tablespoons sweet butter**
4 **tablespoons flour**
1 **cup light cream**
2 **teaspoons vanilla extract**
6 **ounces dark sweet chocolate**
4 **tablespoons brandy**
3 **tablespoons super-fine sugar**
4 **egg yolks**
7 **egg whites**

1. Grease bottom and sides of 1½ quart soufflé dish with the soft butter. Sprinkle with granulated sugar, tipping and shaking the dish to spread the sugar evenly. Turn the dish over and knock out the excess. Set the soufflé dish aside.

2. In a 3 to 4 quart saucepan, melt the sweet butter over low heat. Add the flour to the butter, stirring constantly, and cook for 3 to 5 minutes.

3. In a separate small saucepan, scald the light cream and add vanilla.

4. Add the cream to the butter and flour mixture and cook until it thickens and almost comes to a boil. Cool.

5. In a separate small saucepan melt the chocolate and add the brandy and super-fine sugar. Stir until mixture is smooth. Add to cream mixture. Cover and set aside for 3 to 4 hours. DO NOT REFRIGERATE.

6. When ready to bake soufflé, beat the egg whites in a large mixing bowl until stiff. Fold ¼ of the whites into the chocolate mixture and then fold in the rest until just blended.

7. Place the chocolate mixture into the prepared soufflé dish. Put the soufflé dish in the bottom of a small roasting pan. Fill the pan with boiling water that reaches ½ way up the sides of the soufflé dish. Bake in a preheated 375 degree oven for 50 minutes.

8. While soufflé is baking, in a medium bowl beat together the confectioners' sugar, melted butter, egg yolk, vanilla, and salt. In a separate bowl whip the cream until it forms soft peaks. Fold the whipped cream into the sugar mixture.

9. Remove the soufflé from the oven and serve at once with the Vanilla Sauce. Yield: 6 servings.

This soufflé never fails and is a chocolate lover's delight. The Vanilla Sauce can be made in advance and refrigerated. The sauce will hold for a couple of days without separating.

Vanilla Sauce:
- 1 **cup confectioners' sugar**
- 3 **tablespoons butter, melted**
- 1 **egg yolk**
- ¼ **teaspoon vanilla extract**
- ⅛ **teaspoon salt**
- 1 **cup heavy cream**

Whiskey Bread Pudding

1. Put milk, eggs, vanilla and sugar in blender and mix.

2. Break up bread into small pieces, mix in raisins and place in a well-buttered 9x13 inch baking dish. Pour egg mixture into dish, dot with butter and bake at 350 degrees for 1 hour until very firm. Cool.

3. For the sauce, cream butter and sugar and heat in top of a double boiler until dissolved. Slowly add beaten egg to the mixture, stirring constantly. Cool. Add whiskey.

4. To serve, cut into individual servings, add sauce and heat under broiler. Yield: 8 to 10 servings.

- 1 **loaf of French bread, crumbled**
- 1 **quart milk**
- 4 **eggs, lightly beaten**
- 1¾ **cups sugar**
- 2 **tablespoons vanilla**
- 1 **cup raisins**
- 3 **tablespoons butter**

Whiskey Sauce:
- ¼ **pound butter**
- 1 **cup sugar**
- 1 **egg, well beaten**
- 4 **tablespoons bourbon**

Victorian Cream with Raspberry Sauce and Peaches

1	**cup whipping cream**
½	**cup sugar**
1	**envelope gelatin, softened with 2 tablespoons water**
1	**cup sour cream**
1	**teaspoon vanilla**

Raspberry Sauce:

1	**package frozen raspberries**
1	**teaspoon cornstarch**
⅓	**cup sugar**
	fresh or frozen peaches
	Grand Marnier (optional)

1. In a saucepan combine whipping cream with sugar and cook over low heat stirring constantly until sugar is dissolved. Remove from heat and add gelatin. Mix thoroughly. Stir in sour cream and vanilla.

2. Pour mixture into a lightly oiled 1 pint mold, or six individual molds, and chill until firm.

3. To prepare Raspberry Sauce, thaw and mash raspberries in a food processor or blender. Put through a sieve to remove seeds. Transfer to a saucepan and mix with cornstarch and sugar. Bring to a boil. Set aside. Chill.

4. Unmold Victorian Cream onto a chilled plate(s). Top with Raspberry Sauce. Arrange peach slices around side. Drizzle with Grand Marnier, if desired. Yield: 6 to 8 servings.

Chess Pie

2	**eggs**
1	**cup sugar**
½	**cup butter or margarine**
1	**teaspoon flour**
1	**cup raisins**
1	**cup chopped walnuts**
1	**teaspoon vanilla**
1	**unbaked pie crust**

1. Beat eggs, add sugar and butter and beat well.

2. Mix flour with raisins and nuts, and fold into batter. Add vanilla.

3. Pour into unbaked pie shell. Bake at 350 degrees for 40 to 60 minutes. Wiggle to see if it is firm, if it jiggles, it is not done enough. Watch carefully so as not to overcook. Yield: One 8 to 10 inch pie.

Never Fail Pastry

1. With pastry cutter, mix first 4 ingredients. Cut shortening into flour to the size of peas.

2. In a small bowl, beat water, vinegar and egg. Add to the flour mixture and blend with a fork until dry ingredients are moistened.

3. With hands, mold dough into a ball and chill at least 15 minutes.

4. For pie shells, roll out dough, place in pie tins, and bake at 450 degrees for 12 to 15 minutes, or for tart shells, 8 to 10 minutes. Yield: 4 to 5 single pie crusts.

Dough can be stored in refrigerator up to 3 days, or can be frozen until ready to use. If you freeze it, divide into 4 or 5 equal balls and wrap individually.

4	cups all-purpose flour
1¾	cups shortening (not oil)
1	tablespoon sugar
2	teaspoons salt
½	cup water
1	tablespoon white vinegar
1	egg

PRIZE WINNER • SELMA RAISIN FESTIVAL

Raisin Walnut Pie

1. In a saucepan, combine brown sugar and cornstarch. Stir in raisins, orange peel and juice, lemon peel and juice and cold water. Cook over medium heat until thick and bubbly, cook and stir 1 minute more. Remove from heat and stir in walnuts.

2. Fill pastry-lined 9 inch pie plate with raisin mixture. Add top pie crust and bake in 375 degree oven for 40 minutes. Yield: One 9 inch pie.

Gerald D. Petery

1	cup brown sugar
2	tablespoons cornstarch
2	cups raisins
½	teaspoon shredded orange peel
½	cup orange juice
½	teaspoon shredded lemon peel
2	tablespoons lemon juice
1⅓	cups cold water
½	cup chopped walnuts pastry for pie shell and top

Brandy Pumpkin Pie

1   10 inch deep-dish
    pastry
1   egg white
Filling:
2   cups canned pumpkin
    (16 ounce can)
2   cups whipping cream,
    scalded
1⅓ cups sugar
6   eggs, slightly beaten
½   cup brandy
2   teaspoons cinnamon
2   teaspoons nutmeg
½   teaspoon mace
½   teaspoon ginger
    whipped cream
    (optional)
Pecan Topping:
½   cup chopped pecans
⅓   cup brown sugar

1. Prepare pastry. Line a 10 inch deep-dish pie pan with pastry and brush with egg white. Bake in 325 degree oven until egg white sets, about 5 minutes.

2. Mix filling in order given, and pour into pie pan. (There may be extra filling, this can be baked in a buttered casserole dish.)

3. Bake at 325 degrees for 1 hour or until a knife inserted into center comes out clean.

4. To make Pecan Topping, sprinkle with pecans and shake brown sugar over top. Glaze briefly under broiler. Watch carefully as it will burn quickly at this point. Yield: One 10 inch deep-dish pie.

The pie may be frozen after baking.

There once was a hesitant cook,
Who always abode "by the book"
It said "Baked Alaska";
She lived in Nebraska,
So that recipe she forsook.

Upside-Down Apple Pecan Praline Pie

1. Heat oven to 375 degrees. Combine pecans, brown sugar, and melted butter. Spread on bottom of 9 inch pie pan. Carefully place bottom crust over pecans.

2. In a large bowl, combine apples, flour, sugars, spice, lemon juice and brandy. Mix well to combine; carefully place in pie shell and dot with butter. Put on top crust, seal edges, crimp, and bake at 375 degrees for 40 to 50 minutes. Cool in pan for 5 minutes.

3. Carefully invert pie onto heatproof plate. Cool for an hour before cutting.

4. Combine all topping ingredients and pipe onto border of pie. Yield: One 9 inch pie.

Alberta F. Dunbar

Bottom Layer:
- 1 **cup pecan halves**
- ½ **cup brown sugar, firmly packed**
- ⅓ **cup butter, melted pastry for double crust 9 inch pie**

Filling:
- 6 **Granny Smith apples, peeled and sliced**
- ½ **cup sugar**
- ¼ **cup brown sugar, firmly packed**
- 2 **tablespoons flour**
- 2 **teaspoons apple pie spice**
- 1 **tablespoon lemon juice**
- 2 **tablespoons apple brandy**
- 2 **tablespoons sweet butter**

Topping:
- 1 **(8 ounce) package cream cheese**
- 2 **tablespoons sour cream**
- 1 **tablespoon sugar**
- ½ **teaspoon brandy extract**

Grandma's Apple Slices

Crust:
- 2 **cups flour**
- ½ **teaspoon salt**
- ⅔ **cup margarine**
- 2 **egg yolks**
- 1 **teaspoon lemon juice**
- ¼ **cup water**

Filling:
- 4-6 **tart apples, peeled and sliced**
- 1 **cup sugar**
- 2 **tablespoons flour**
- ½ **teaspoon cinnamon**

Frosting:
- 1 **cup powdered sugar**
- 2 **tablespoons butter**
- ¼ **teaspoon vanilla**
- 2 **tablespoons milk**

1. For crust sift flour with salt, cut in margarine, set aside. Shake together yolks, lemon juice and water. Sprinkle over flour blend. Knead lightly until it sticks together. Divide into two parts, one slightly larger than the other. Roll smaller portion to fit a 9x13 inch baking dish. Place in dish.

2. For filling combine sugar, flour and cinnamon. Arrange apple slices in baking dish, and sprinkle with sugar mixture.

3. Roll remaining dough to fit top. Seal edges and cut steam vents. Bake at 400 degrees for 30 to 40 minutes, or until light brown.

4. Mix frosting ingredients and frost when pie is cool. Yield: 12 servings.

Spirited Apple Crisp

- 5 **cups peeled and sliced tart-sweet apples**
- 1 **teaspoon cinnamon**
- 1 **teaspoon cloves**
- ½ **teaspoon nutmeg**
- 1 **teaspoon lemon juice**
- 1 **teaspoon finely grated lemon rind**
- 1 **teaspoon grated orange rind**
- 1 **jigger Grand Marnier**
- 1 **jigger amaretto**
- ½ **cup granulated sugar**
- ¾ **cup brown sugar**
- ⅓ **cup flour**
- ¼ **teaspoon salt**
- ½ **cup butter**
- 1 **cup chopped walnuts**

1. Arrange apple slices in buttered 9 inch pie plate.

2. Sprinkle cinnamon, cloves, nutmeg, lemon and orange rinds, lemon juice and both liqueurs on top of the apples.

3. In separate bowl mix sugars, flour, salt and butter with a pastry blender until crumbly. Add walnuts. Spread mixture over apples. Bake at 350 degrees for 1 hour. Yield: 8 servings.

Indulge Today, Diet Tomorrow Trifle

1. Mix sugar and yolks in blender for 1 minute; add vanilla and blend 1 minute longer. Add the cream cheese and blend until smooth. Chill.

2. Beat whipping cream until stiff; add cream cheese mix. Chill.

3. Dunk cake strips into diluted espresso, coating all sides slightly. Arrange a layer of cake on the bottom of a clear trifle dish. Sprinkle with ½ of the shaved chocolate. Top with ½ of the cream cheese mix, and arrange 1 cup of sliced berries. Top with remaining cake strips, shaved chocolate, cream cheese and sliced berries. Cover tightly and chill until serving time. Yield: 8 to 10 servings.

Debbie Del Toro

1 cup sugar
6 egg yolks
2 teaspoons pure vanilla
1 (8 ounce) package cream cheese, softened
1½ cups whipping cream, chilled
1 tablespoon instant espresso powder, dissolved in 1¼ cups hot water, cooled
1 (12 ounce) prepared pound cake, cut into strips (1x3x½ inch)
10 ounces shaved white chocolate
2 cups sliced fresh strawberries

The pudding supporters on hand
Were making their final demand;
"We want a real egg;
You dare not renege."
It sounded like
*   "custard's last stand."*

Sandtorte with Raspberry Puree

Cake:
- 1 **cup unsalted butter, softened**
- 3 **cups sugar**
- 6 **eggs**
- 1 **cup sour cream**
- 3 **cups flour**
- ¼ **teaspoon baking powder**
- 2 **teaspoons vanilla grated zest of 1 orange (only the colored portion of orange rind) powdered sugar (optional)**

Topping:
- 3 **baskets raspberries, divided**
- 1 **tablespoon cognac sugar to taste**

1. Cream the butter well in large bowl with mixer. Blend in the sugar, ½ cup at a time. Add the eggs, one at a time, blending well after each addition. Blend in sour cream and beat until light and fluffy.

2. Sift the flour, measure and sift again with the baking powder. Add flour in 4 or 5 parts, mixing well after each addition. Add vanilla and orange zest.

3. Pour batter into a well-buttered Bundt pan. Bake at 325 degrees for 60 to 70 minutes, or until it tests done when toothpick inserted in center of cake comes out clean. Cool on rack for 10 minutes then remove from pan and cool completely. Wrap tightly in plastic or foil and leave at room temperature. (Best if made 1 day ahead of serving.)

4. In blender or food processor, puree 2 baskets of raspberries, lightly coated with cognac and sugar to taste. Sieve to remove seeds. Let stand, covered, for several hours to blend the flavors.

5. Sprinkle top of cake with powdered sugar, if desired. Serve sliced cake with raspberry puree. Garnish with remaining basket of whole berries or orange slices. Yield: 12 to 16 servings.

Tiramisu ("Pick Me Up")

1. Beat egg whites until stiff peaks form. Put aside. Beat egg yolks with sugar until thick and pale yellow. Fold in mascarpone and egg whites until thoroughly incorporated.

2. In a medium-sized bowl, combine the espresso and Kahlúa. Dip the ladyfingers into this mixture very quickly, one at a time. Place a layer of ladyfingers in a decorative bowl or 10x14 inch glass dish. Spread ½ the mascarpone mixture evenly over the ladyfingers, top with ½ the hazelnuts and sprinkle with cocoa (through a fine-mesh strainer). Repeat with another layer of ladyfingers and mascarpone, nuts and cocoa.

3. Cover with plastic wrap and refrigerate for several hours (or overnight). Just before serving, shave some chocolate with a vegetable peeler and sprinkle over the cake. Garnish with raspberries if desired. Yield: 12 or more servings.

Freezes well.

8 **large egg whites, beaten until stiff**
8 **large egg yolks**
½ **cup sugar**
1 **pound mascarpone cheese**
2-3 **cups cold espresso**
¼ **cup Kahlúa**
2 **packages imported ladyfingers (48)**
½ **cup cocoa powder (unsweetened)**
½ **cup hazelnuts, roasted, skinned and chopped fine (optional)**
semi-sweet chocolate for garnish
raspberries for garnish (optional)

Elegant Strawberry Tiramisu

1 **package commercial ladyfingers (split)**
3 **tablespoons strawberry liqueur**
1 **tablespoon instant espresso powder or granules**
2 **(8 ounce) packages cream cheese, preferably low fat**
⅔ **cup powdered sugar**
1 **basket fresh strawberries, or 1½ cups frozen, thawed and drained**
¾ **cup freshly brewed strong coffee, preferably espresso, room temperature**
3 **tablespoons sugar additional powdered sugar Strawberry Sauce**

Strawberry Sauce:
1 **(10 ounce) package frozen strawberries in syrup, thawed**
2 **tablespoons strawberry liqueur**

1. For sauce, puree strawberries and syrup in a blender or food processor. Strain into small bowl to remove seeds. Stir in strawberry liqueur. Can be prepared 2 days ahead. Cover and refrigerate.

2. Place ladyfingers in an 8x8 inch square pan, flat side up, to cover bottom of pan.

3. Combine strawberry liqueur and instant espresso in small bowl. Stir until espresso dissolves. Using an electric mixer, blend cream cheese and ⅔ cup powdered sugar and beat until light and fluffy. Add strawberry liqueur and espresso to mixture and blend well. Fold in slightly crushed strawberries. Let stand at room temperature.

4. Combine coffee and 3 tablespoons sugar. Stir until sugar dissolves. Spoon coffee mixture over ladyfingers, using ½ of coffee. Pile filling atop ladyfingers using ½ of the mixture. Place ladyfingers atop filling and repeat once more, ending with ladyfingers atop mixture and using all of the coffee mixture. Sprinkle with powdered sugar. Spoon strawberry sauce over 6 individual portions. Yield: 6 servings.

Vivian Ebert

Lemon Cake

1. Cream margarine and sugar. Add beaten eggs. Blend well.

2. Sift together flour, salt and baking soda. Add to egg mixture. Blend well.

3. Add buttermilk and lemon rind. Mix until blended.

4. Grease and flour a 9x5x3 inch loaf pan. Pour batter into pan and bake in a 350 degree oven for 1 hour and 15 minutes. When done and while still hot, make holes all over loaf with a toothpick. Drizzle with lemon juice mixed with sugar. Cool and serve. Yield: One 9x5x3 inch loaf.

¾ **cup margarine**
1½ **cups sugar**
3 **eggs, beaten**
2¼ **cups flour**
¼ **teaspoon salt**
¼ **teaspoon baking soda**
¾ **cup buttermilk**
1 **lemon rind, grated**
  juice of 2 lemons
¼ **cup sugar**

Orange Slice Cake

1. Chop or slice nuts, dates, and candy. Add coconut. Pour melted butter over the mixture and let stand while preparing batter.

2. Beat eggs, add sugar and other ingredients.

3. Combine and mix well with nut and candy mixture. Bake in a greased tube or Bundt pan in a 300 degree oven for 1 hour and 45 minutes to 2 hours.

4. Cut into fairly small slices. Serve plain or with whipped cream. Yield: 18 to 20 servings.

2 **cups pecans or walnuts**
1 **(8 ounce) package pitted dates**
1 **pound candy orange slices (gum drop)**
1 **cup butter, melted**
4 **eggs**
1½ **cups sugar**
½ **cup buttermilk**
1 **teaspoon soda**
2 **cups flour**
1 **(7 ounce) can or package flaked coconut**

PRIZE WINNER • SELMA RAISIN FESTIVAL

Raw Raisin Apple Cake

2 cups flour
2 cups sugar *too much !*
½ cup oil
2 beaten eggs
2 teaspoons cinnamon
½ teaspoon salt
2 teaspoons baking soda
½ teaspoon baking powder
dash nutmeg *(pecans)*
1 cup chopped walnuts
4 cups thinly sliced, peeled apples
¾ cup raisins

Frosting:
1 cup whipping cream
1 tablespoon vanilla
3 tablespoons sugar
¼ teaspoon cinnamon

1. Mix all ingredients in order given. Beat until smooth. Pour into an oiled 9x13 inch pan and bake in a 350 degree oven for 25 to 30 minutes. Cool.

2. To make Frosting, beat whipping cream. Add vanilla, sugar and cinnamon. Frost cake. Yield: 15 to 18 servings.

Ruth B. Ekberg

add.
1 c. shredded coconut
use 1 c. less sugar.

Fantastic and Easy Fruit Torte

1 cup sugar
½ cup butter, softened
1¼ cups cake flour
1 teaspoon baking soda
pinch of salt
2 eggs
fruit (use whatever is in season; pears, apples, peaches or plums), peeled and sliced

Topping:
2 tablespoons sugar
1 tablespoon cinnamon
2 teaspoons lemon juice

1. In food processor or blender, cream butter and sugar. Add the flour, baking soda, salt and eggs. Mix well.

2. Butter and flour an 8½ inch springform pan. Spread batter in pan. Arrange fruit in spiral pattern pushing down into batter. Combine the sugar, cinnamon and lemon juice and sprinkle over the fruit.

3. Bake 1 hour in 350 degree oven. Delicious with ice cream. Can be made ahead and frozen. Yield: 6 to 8 servings.

Carrot Cake With Cream Cheese Frosting

1. Sift together flour, baking powder, baking soda, salt and cinnamon. Set aside. Grate carrots.

2. Blend sugar and oil. Add eggs one at a time, mixing thoroughly after each. Add carrots. Blend thoroughly. Gradually add sifted dry ingredients then nuts, combining thoroughly.

3. Pour into 3 greased, floured and paper lined 8 or 9 inch round cake pans. Bake in 300 degree oven for 50 minutes. Test with a toothpick. Cool.

4. To make Cream Cheese Frosting, use an electric mixer to thoroughly combine butter and cream cheese. Gradually add powdered sugar and beat until light and fluffy. Stir in vanilla. Spread onto completely cooled cake. Yield: 12 servings.

2 cups flour
2 teaspoons baking powder
2 teaspoons baking soda
1 teaspoon salt
1 tablespoon cinnamon
3 cups grated raw carrots
2 cups sugar
1½ cups corn oil
4 eggs
1½ cups nuts, coarsely chopped

Cream Cheese Frosting:
¼ cup butter, softened
1 (8 ounce) package cream cheese, softened
1 pound box powdered sugar
1½ teaspoons vanilla

Angel Almond Cake

1. Mix first 5 ingredients together until well blended.

2. Press into two 9 inch pie plates that have been greased and lined with wax paper. Spread each with beaten egg white. Sprinkle with sliced almonds and sugar. Bake in 325 degree oven for 25 to 30 minutes. Yield: 12 servings.

Freezes well.

1 cup butter, softened
1½ cups sugar
1 egg plus 1 egg yolk
2½ cups flour
1½ teaspoons almond extract
1 egg white
½ cup sliced almonds
¼ cup sugar

Chocolate Strawberry Decadence

1 cup toasted hazelnuts or almonds, finely ground

6 tablespoons unsweetened cocoa powder

¾ cup butter, room temperature

1 cup sugar

¼ cup brown sugar

4 eggs, room temperature

½ teaspoon vanilla

½ cup fresh strawberries, halved

⅓ cup strawberry preserves
fresh strawberries for garnish

Ganache:

¼ cup heavy cream

6 ounces semi-sweet chocolate chips

1. Combine nuts and cocoa until well mixed.

2. Cream butter and sugars until fluffy. Beat in eggs one at a time until very light. Beat in vanilla and fold in nut mixture, then strawberries.

3. Butter an 8½ inch spring-form pan and bake at 350 degrees for 35 to 45 minutes. Cool completely.

4. Remove cake from pan and spread strawberry preserves on top.

5. Make Ganache by bringing cream to a boil in a small saucepan. Remove from heat and add chocolate chips. Stir until smooth and cool 5 minutes. Pour Ganache over top of cake and let drizzle down sides. Garnish with fresh strawberries. Yield: 6 to 8 servings.

Lisa Bucher

Party Chocolate Cheesecake

1. Combine crust ingredients in blender or food processor. Pat into bottom and sides of a buttered 8 inch spring-form pan.

2. Filling: beat cream cheese until smooth. Add eggs and blend. Melt chocolate chips in microwave or over hot water. Add chocolate, sour cream, liqueur and cinnamon to cream cheese mixture and mix until blended.

3. Pour filling into crust and bake in preheated 350 degree oven for 50 to 55 minutes. Cool slightly, then chill 1½ hours or overnight. Before serving, top with Raspberry Glaze (optional) and drizzle Sugar Glaze over all, in a linear pattern. Garnish with fresh raspberries, mint or citrus leaves and/or sliced citrus.

4. To make Raspberry Glaze, bring raspberries to a boil in microwave (in a covered glass container) or in a heavy saucepan on the stove. Add sugar, salt and liqueur. Mix cornstarch, water and coloring in a bowl; gradually add to raspberry mixture. Bring to a boil again, stirring until thickened. Remove from heat, cool, spread on top of cooled cheesecake.

5. For Sugar Glaze, gradually add liquid to sugar until glaze will drizzle in a thin line when tipped from a spoon. Decorate cheesecake in a crisscross linear pattern. Yield: 12 to 16 servings.

Crust:
- 1½ cups chocolate wafer crumbs
- 1 cup slivered almonds, chopped
- ¼ cup sugar
- 6 tablespoons butter, warm
- ½ teaspoon grated orange rind

Filling:
- 2 (8 ounce) packages cream cheese, softened
- 3 eggs
- 8 ounces semi-sweet chocolate chips
- 2 cups sour cream
- ¼ cup orange flavored liqueur
- ¾ teaspoon cinnamon (optional)

Raspberry Glaze:
- 1 (10 ounce) package frozen raspberries, thawed and pureed
- ¼ cup sugar, or to taste
- ¼ teaspoon salt
- 1 tablespoon orange flavored liqueur
- ¼ cup cornstarch
- ½ cup cold water
  red food coloring (optional)

Sugar Glaze:
  sifted powdered sugar
  water or milk

Marvelous Mud Cake

1 cup butter, softened
1 cup sugar
2 eggs
⅓ cup cocoa
1½ cups flour
1½ teaspoons vanilla
½ package miniature
  marshmallows

Topping:
1 cup butter
⅓ cup cocoa
1 pound powdered sugar
½ cup evaporated milk

1. Cream butter and sugar. Add eggs and blend. Add cocoa and flour and mix well. Add vanilla.

2. Place in a greased and floured 9x13 inch pan. Bake in a 350 degree oven for 20 minutes.

3. Remove from oven and cover top with miniature marshmallows.

4. Return to oven until marshmallows are lightly browned, 5 to 10 minutes. Remove from oven and cool.

5. For topping, melt butter and stir in cocoa. Add powdered sugar and mix well. Add evaporated milk slowly, mixing until well blended. Pour over marshmallows. Cool overnight. Cut into 1x1 inch pieces. Yield: 4 to 5 dozen.

Wine Poached Pears

1. Use a saucepan that is just large enough to hold the 4 pears side by side.

2. Combine the wine, sugar, anise, cinnamon and lemon in the saucepan; bring to a boil, stirring until the sugar is dissolved.

3. Remove core from the wide end of the pear, leaving the stem in place. Carefully peel pears and set pears into boiling syrup. Cover and boil 8 to 12 minutes. Turn fruit 2 to 3 times so that all the pear has a cooking time in the syrup.

4. Transfer fruit to serving dish with slotted spoon. Boil syrup at high heat, uncovered, until reduced to ⅔ cup. Pour hot syrup over and around pears. Serve warm or at room temperature. Yield: 4 servings.

4   **large firm Bartlett pears**
1   **cup plus 2 tablespoons dry red California wine**
⅔   **cup sugar**
¼   **teaspoon anise seed**
2   **sticks whole cinnamon**
2   **thin unpeeled lemon slices**

Toffee Bars

1. Preheat oven to 350 degrees. Cream butter, sugar and vanilla. Add flour and salt. Mix in nuts and chocolate chips.

2. Spread onto jelly-roll pan and bake for 20 minutes. Cut into squares immediately. Cool in pan. Yield: 2 dozen bars.

1   **cup butter**
1   **cup brown sugar**
1   **teaspoon vanilla extract**
1   **cup flour**
    dash of salt
6   **ounces chocolate chips**
1   **cup chopped walnuts**

Apricot Ribbon Cookies

1 cup unsalted butter, at room temperature
½ cup sugar
1 egg yolk
2½ cups flour
¼ teaspoon almond extract
½ cup apricot jam, melted

Icing:
½ cup powdered sugar
2 tablespoons sherry

1. Cream butter and sugar until fluffy. Mix in egg yolk, beat in flour and extract.

2. Shape into ½ inch diameter ropes on ungreased cookie sheet. Using finger, press a ¼ inch groove into the center of each rope. Bake in pre-heated 375 degree oven for 10 minutes or until they just begin to brown. Remove from oven, fill grooves with melted jam and return to oven until golden, about 5 to 10 minutes. Cool 5 minutes.

3. For icing, dissolve sugar in sherry and drizzle on with a spoon in zigzag pattern. Cut diagonally into 1 inch pieces and cool on rack. Store airtight.

Richard N. Kelly

Chocolate Peanut Butter Bars

1 cup peanut butter, divided
½ cup margarine, softened
1 cup brown sugar, firmly packed
1 egg
1 teaspoon vanilla
2 cups sifted flour
¼ teaspoon salt
1 (6 ounce) package semi-sweet chocolate chips, melted

1. Cream ½ cup peanut butter, margarine and sugar. Beat in egg and vanilla. Sift flour and salt together and blend into batter. Spread dough onto a buttered 15½x10½x1 inch baking sheet (using a large fork makes spreading the dough easier). Bake in 325 degree oven for 20 to 25 minutes.

2. For frosting combine melted chocolate chips with the remaining ½ cup of peanut butter, blend well and immediately spread the frosting over bars. Cut while still warm (important as the bars will crumble if sliced when cooled). Yield: 4 dozen normal or 2 dozen teenage portions.

Walnut Cherry Shortbread Bars

1. Cream butter, shortening, egg yolk, sugar and vanilla together. Add flour and mix until smooth.

2. Pat the dough evenly on a buttered cookie sheet (about 10x13 inch). Brush top lightly with egg white. Sprinkle with chopped walnuts and gently press into the dough. Sprinkle the chopped cherries on top.

3. Bake in a 350 degree oven for 20 minutes, or until golden. Remove from the oven and cut into rectangles, squares, or diamonds while still warm. Yield: 5 dozen 1x2 inch pieces or 30 2x2 inch squares.

This is a great recipe for a cookie exchange or any time you need a quantity of easy to make cookies.

½	cup butter, softened
¼	cup vegetable shortening
1	egg yolk
¾	cup sugar
1¾	cups flour, sifted
1	teaspoon vanilla
1	egg white, lightly beaten
1¼	cups walnuts, chopped
10	maraschino cherries, chopped

PRIZE WINNER • CHERRY FESTIVAL

Almond Bark Cookies

1. Melt almond bark and peanut butter. Stir well.

2. Combine remaining ingredients in a large bowl. Add almond bark mixture and mix well. Drop by the spoonful onto wax paper. Let set several hours. Place in container with wax paper between layers.

Keep in refrigerator or may be frozen.

Dicky Krenz

3	cups Captain Crunch cereal
2	cups crisp rice cereal
3	cups cut-up California walnuts
1	cup peanut butter
1	cup cut-up California maraschino cherries, well drained
2	pounds white chocolate (almond bark)
1	large package tiny multi-colored marshmallows

Granola Bars

½ cup butter, margarine or vegetable oil
1½ cups packed light or dark brown sugar
2 eggs
¾ cup flour
1 cup instant oatmeal
1½ cups coconut
1 teaspoon baking powder
½ teaspoon salt
½ teaspoon vanilla
½ cup coarsely chopped walnuts
½ cup raisins (optional)
½ cup other nuts (optional)
chocolate or butterscotch chips (optional)

1. Heat oven to 350 degrees. If using butter or margarine, melt over low heat. Remove from heat, stir into sugar and let cool. Add eggs.

2. Mix flour, oatmeal, baking powder and salt together and add to butter. Stir in vanilla, coconut and nuts. Add optional ingredients as desired. Spread in well-greased 8x8x2 inch pan. Bake for 25 to 35 minutes. Do not overbake. Cut when cool. Yield: 18 bars.

If doubling the recipe, use a 9x13 inch pan.

There was an old vicar at Trinity
Who loved to expound on infinity;
At rectory teas
He rambled at ease
Over angel food cake and divinity.

Pecan Bars

1. Sift together flour and sugar. Using a food processor or pastry blender, cut butter into flour to form fine crumbs. Pat crust into a greased 9x13 inch baking pan. Be sure to distribute evenly. Bake for 20 minutes in a 350 degree oven.

2. While crust is baking, blend together the melted butter, brown sugar, honey and cream. Add pecans and stir until completely coated. Cover crust with topping and return to oven for another 20 to 25 minutes.

3. Using a thin bladed knife, rinsed frequently in warm water, cut around the edges of the pan and slice the bars while still warm, before the topping hardens. Yield: 3 dozen.

Freezes well.

2 **cups flour**
⅔ **cup powdered sugar**
1 **cup unsalted butter, softened**

Pecan Topping:
⅔ **cup unsalted butter, melted**
½ **cup brown sugar**
½ **cup honey**
3 **tablespoons heavy cream**
3½ **cups chopped pecans**

Sandwich Fruit Cookies

1½ cups flour
1 teaspoon soda
½ teaspoon salt
1¾ cups oatmeal
1 cup brown sugar, packed
¾ cup margarine
Raisin Filling:
1 cup raisins
¼ cup sugar
1 teaspoon lemon juice
2 tablespoons cornstarch
¼ cup water

1. Mix first 5 ingredients. Add margarine and blend as for pastry. Pat ½ of the mixture into a 9x13 inch lightly buttered pan. Set aside.

2. Combine filling ingredients except cornstarch and water in a saucepan. Add water to cover. Simmer 5 minutes. Mix cornstarch with ¼ cup water. Add to raisin mixture and cook until it becomes thick and clear, about 2 minutes.

3. Place filling on top of crust. Top with rest of oatmeal mixture.

4. Bake in 350 degree oven for 30 to 35 minutes. Yield: 1 to 2 dozen.

Very good served warm or cold with a scoop of ice cream or plain as a cookie.

Frosted Pumpkin Cookies

1 cup shortening
1 cup sugar
1½ cups canned pumpkin
1 egg
2 cups flour
1 teaspoon soda
1 teaspoon cinnamon
1 teaspoon salt
1 cup butterscotch bits
1 cup nuts
1 cup raisins
Frosting:
3 tablespoons butter
4 teaspoons milk
½ cup brown sugar
1 cup powdered sugar
¾ teaspoon vanilla

1. Preheat oven. Cream shortening and sugar. Add pumpkin and egg. Combine flour, soda, cinnamon and salt. Mix into creamed mixture. Stir in butterscotch bits, nuts and raisins.

2. Spoon dough onto ungreased cookie sheet. Bake for 10 to 12 minutes in a 375 degree oven.

3. For frosting, combine butter, milk and brown sugar in saucepan. Cook until dissolved. Cool and then stir in powdered sugar and vanilla. Frost cookies while hot. Yield: 4 to 5 dozen cookies.

Brandy Apple Squares

1. Pare, core and shred apples. Add brandy and let sit overnight.

2. Cream eggs, sugar and oil until fluffy. Stir in apples. Add nuts if desired.

3. Sift together flour, soda, spices and salt. Lightly fold into the apple mixture until well blended.

4. Grease and flour a 9x13 inch pan. Bake in 350 degree oven for 50 to 60 minutes. Test at 50 minutes. Cool before adding frosting.

5. For frosting, cream together powdered sugar, cream cheese, butter, vanilla and salt until smoothly blended. Frost cooled cake. Cut into squares and serve. Yield: 32 small or 16 large squares.

4   apples
½   cup brandy
2   eggs
2   cups sugar
½   cup oil
2   cups flour
2   teaspoons soda
2   teaspoons cinnamon
1   teaspoon nutmeg
½   teaspoon cloves
1   scant teaspoon salt
1   cup chopped walnuts
    or pecans (optional)

Frosting:

1½   cups powdered sugar
1   (8 ounce) package
    cream cheese
3   tablespoons butter
1   teaspoon vanilla
    dash of salt

Kahlúa Party Bars

1½	**cups graham cracker crumbs**
1	**cup chopped toasted almonds**
½	**cup plus 1½ tablespoons butter, divided**
¼	**cup granulated sugar**
⅓	**cup cocoa**
1	**egg**
1½	**teaspoons vanilla**
6	**tablespoons Kahlúa, divided**
6	**tablespoons unsalted butter**
1	**tablespoon milk**
1¾	**cups powdered sugar**
4	**ounces semi-sweet chocolate**

1. Combine graham cracker crumbs and almonds in a 7x11x1½ inch baking pan.

2. In a saucepan, melt ½ cup butter. Add granulated sugar, cocoa, egg and vanilla. Cook until thickened, stirring constantly. Pour over crumb mixture and mix. Press down. Sprinkle with 3 tablespoons of Kahlúa. Place in freezer.

3. Cream together unsalted butter, milk and 3 tablespoons of Kahlúa. Slowly add powdered sugar. Mix until smooth. Spread on chilled graham layer. Freeze.

4. Melt 1½ tablespoons butter and semi-sweet chocolate over low heat. Blend. Spread over chilled powdered sugar layer. Work quickly. Slice into bars. Yield: 35 to 40 bars.

Pineapple Raisin Cookies

1. Boil water and raisins together for 5 minutes, then cool.

2. Cream butter and sugar. Add eggs and beat well. Add vanilla, raisins and pineapple. Add dry ingredients and nuts. Blend well.

3. Drop by spoonfuls onto greased baking sheets. Bake 12 to 15 minutes in 350 degree oven. Yield: 6 dozen cookies.

Louise Khasigian

1	cup water
2	cups raisins
1	cup butter, softened
2	cups sugar
3	eggs
1	teaspoon vanilla
¼	teaspoon nutmeg
1	cup crushed pineapple, drained
5	cups flour
1	teaspoon baking soda
1	teaspoon baking powder
1	teaspoon salt
1½	teaspoons cinnamon
1	cup chopped walnuts

Chocolate-Peanut Butter Chip Cookies

1. Cream together butter, sugar and brown sugar, blend in eggs and vanilla. Add flour, baking powder, baking soda and salt. Mix very well. Stir in corn flakes, oatmeal, coconut, chips and nuts.

2. Using a small ice cream scoop, place dough on ungreased cookie sheet. Bake in a 350 degree oven for 13 to 15 minutes. Yield: 6 to 8 dozen cookies.

2	cups butter or margarine, softened
2	cups sugar
2	cups brown sugar
5	eggs
2	teaspoons vanilla
4	cups flour
2	teaspoons baking powder
2	teaspoons baking soda
1	teaspoon salt
3	cups corn flakes
1	(3½ ounce) can coconut
1	(12 ounce) package chocolate chips
1	(12 ounce) package peanut butter chips
1½	cups walnuts, chopped

Caramel Oatmeal Bars

1¼ **cups plus 3 tablespoons flour, divided**
1¼ **cups rolled oats**
1 **cup brown sugar, firmly packed**
½ **teaspoon soda**
¼ **teaspoon salt**
¾ **cup butter or margarine, melted**
1½-2 **cups chocolate chips**
1-1½ **cups chopped pecans or walnuts**
1-1¼ **cups caramel ice cream topping**

1. In large mixer bowl combine 1¼ cups flour with rolled oats, brown sugar, soda, salt and butter to form coarse crumbs. Press ⅔ of crumbs into the bottom of 7x11 inch pan. Bake in 350 degree oven for 10 minutes. Remove from oven.

2. Sprinkle the chocolate chips and nuts over crumb crust, using as many chips and nuts as needed to cover. Depending on which brand of caramel topping you use, you may need to thicken the topping with up to 3 tablespoons flour. Pour the thick caramel over the chocolate and nuts, crisscrossing the pan to distribute as evenly as possible. Sprinkle the remaining crumbs over all to form a topping. Return to oven and bake for 15 to 20 minutes until golden. Cut into bars. Serve warm or cold. Yield: 16 to 20 bars.

Filo-Nut Dessert Fingers

1. Combine nuts, sugar, orange peel, cinnamon and cloves; mix thoroughly. Place 1 sheet of filo on a board and brush lightly with a scant tablespoon of melted butter. Top with a second sheet of filo and brush again with butter. Sprinkle with ¼ of the nut mixture.

2. With a sharp knife, cut the filo rectangle lengthwise into thirds, then cut each across into halves. Beginning with the short ends, roll each loosely into a log. Repeat with remaining filo sheets.

3. Place logs slightly apart on an ungreased 10x15 inch baking sheet. Brush tops with butter then sprinkle with sugar. Bake in 300 degree oven for 20 to 25 minutes or until golden. Cool completely.

4. In a 1 quart saucepan, combine chocolate chips and butter. Stir over very low heat until melted. Drizzle each filo-nut log with chocolate icing. Yield: 2 dozen fingers.

1 **cup finely chopped walnuts**
½ **cup sugar**
2 **teaspoons grated orange peel**
½ **teaspoon ground cinnamon**
¼ **teaspoon ground cloves**
8 **sheets filo dough**
⅔ **cup melted butter**
2 **teaspoons sugar**
Topping:
⅔ **cup semi-sweet chocolate baking chips**
2 **teaspoons butter**

Chocolate Hazelnut Biscotti

1 cup hazelnuts (or roasted almonds)
½ cup butter
¾ cup sugar
3 eggs
2 teaspoons vanilla (or anise, if using almonds)
3 cups flour, may need up to an additional ½ cup
1 tablespoon baking powder
½ teaspoon salt
1 cup semi-sweet chocolate chips

1. Roast hazelnuts in 350 degree oven for 15 to 20 minutes, shaking occasionally and watching carefully so as not to burn them. Put nuts in a clean dish towel and rub with the cloth to remove skin. Chop coarsely.

2. Beat butter and sugar together until light and fluffy. Add eggs, one at time, beating well after each addition. Stir in vanilla.

3. Sift together flour, baking powder and salt; add to above mixture. Mix in nuts and stir well to combine. Turn mixture out on well-floured board and knead well. Divide into 6 parts. Roll each part 1½ inches thick and place 2 inches apart on ungreased baking sheet. Flatten slightly.

4. Bake in 350 degree oven for 15 to 20 minutes. Let cool, then slice diagonally into ¾ inch slices. Bake another 10 to 15 minutes ("biscotti" means "twice cooked"). Place cookies on racks to cool.

5. Melt chocolate chips and spread chocolate mixture on tops of cooled cookies. Yield: 25 to 30 cookies.

Chocolate Covered Cherry Treats

1. Soak cherries in brandy for 30 minutes, and drain well; if not using brandy, just drain cherry juice from cherries.

2. Cream butter, sugar and vanilla. Blend in flour until dough is mixed. Break dough into marble-sized pieces and flatten. Wrap each piece of dough completely around cherries. Place on cookie sheets and bake 8 to 10 minutes in a 350 degree oven. Cool.

2. Combine topping ingredients and heat slowly until melted. Place cookies on a rack over waxed paper, spoon topping over cookies, reusing amount that drips onto the waxed paper. Yield: 40 treats.

1 (10 ounce) jar maraschino cherries (about 40)
½ cup brandy, if desired
½ cup butter
½ cup powdered sugar
½ teaspoon vanilla
1 cup flour

Chocolate Topping:
1 (6 ounce) package chocolate chips
¼ cup light corn syrup
1 tablespoon water

Candied Almonds

1. In a black iron frying pan, using a large spoon, mix ingredients together. Cook over medium-high heat stirring constantly. Mixture will turn to sugar, then syrup again. When the mixture begins to turn to sugar again, remove from stove and spread on a cookie sheet. In about 1 minute, run a table knife through to separate. Do the same thing in about 3 minutes, then in 5 minutes, to keep them from sticking. Yield: 3 cups almonds.

½ cup boiling water
1½ cups granulated sugar
3 cups almond meats with skins left on

English Toffee

1½ **cups chopped walnuts and toasted almonds (proportions to taste)**
2 **(8 ounce) milk chocolate bars**
2 **cups sugar**
1 **pound butter**

1. Butter a 12 inch or 9x13 inch cake pan. Sprinkle with ¾ cup of nuts. Shave ¾ of one chocolate bar over nuts and set aside.

2. Place the sugar and butter in a heavy saucepan. Cook over medium to high heat and bring to a boil. Stir and scrape sides and bottom of pan often to keep from burning. When candy thermometer reads slightly under 300 degrees and mixture is a caramel color, remove thermometer.

3. Pour hot mixture over nuts and chocolate layer in cake pan. Shave remaining chocolate over hot mixture. When chocolate begins to melt, spread with knife and sprinkle with remaining nuts. Press into chocolate layer. Cool and break into pieces. Yield: 3 pounds of candy.

Peanut Butter Bon Bons

2 **cups powdered sugar**
1 **cup graham cracker crumbs, finely crushed**
½ **cup chopped pecans**
½ **cup coconut, finely chopped**
½ **cup margarine**
½ **cup peanut butter**
1½ **cups chocolate chips**
1 **tablespoon vegetable shortening**

1. Combine sugar, graham cracker crumbs, pecans and coconut in a large bowl.

2. Melt margarine and peanut butter in small saucepan and add to sugar mixture, mixing well. Shape into 1 inch balls.

3. Melt chocolate chips with vegetable shortening. Using toothpicks, dip the balls into the chocolate mixture. Place on waxed paper covered cookie sheet. Cool in refrigerator. Yield: 3½ dozen.

Freezes well.

Chocolate Ricotta Pie

1. Generously grease a 10 inch pie pan. Bring water and shortening to a boil in a pan. Add flour and salt all at once. Stir and cook until it leaves the side and forms a ball. Remove from heat and cool slightly. Beat eggs one at a time until smooth. Spread mixture evenly on bottom of pie pan. Bake in 400 degree oven about 35 minutes or until golden. Cool slightly.

2. Mix Ricotta Filling ingredients until completely blended. Pour over prepared pie shell.

3. To prepare Chocolate Pudding, in a saucepan, combine sugar, cornstarch, salt and chocolate. Gradually stir in milk. Cook and stir 2 minutes. Remove from heat. Stir small amount of hot mixture into yolks, immediately return to hot mixture. Cook 2 minutes, stirring constantly. Remove from heat. Add butter and vanilla. Mix and then pour over Ricotta Filling.

4. Garnish with 2 tablespoons of ground toasted almonds and add 4 or 5 halved maraschino cherries on top. Yield: 10 to 12 servings.

Joann Alton

Cream Puff Shell:
- ½ cup water
- ¼ cup shortening
- ½ cup flour
- dash salt
- 2 eggs

Ricotta Filling:
- 1½ pounds ricotta cheese
- 2¼ cups powdered sugar
- 2½ tablespoons grated milk chocolate
- 2¼ teaspoons vanilla
- 1 teaspoon cinnamon

Chocolate Pudding:
- 1 cup sugar
- 3 tablespoons cornstarch
- ¼ teaspoon salt
- 2 (1 ounce) squares unsweetened chocolate
- 2¼ cups milk
- 3 slightly beaten egg yolks
- 2 tablespoons butter
- 1 teaspoon vanilla
- 2 tablespoons ground toasted almonds, for garnish
- 4-5 maraschino cherries, halved, for garnish

Cassata Alla Siciliana

fresh pound cake,
home-baked or
purchased
1 pound ricotta cheese
2 tablespoons whipping
cream
¼ cup sugar
3 tablespoons Strega or
orange liqueur
3 tablespoons chopped
mixed candied fruit
2 ounces semi-sweet
chocolate, coarsely
chopped

Frosting:
12 ounces semi-sweet
chocolate cut in small
pieces
¾ cup strong black coffee
½ pound unsalted butter,
cut in ½ inch pieces
and thoroughly chilled

1. With a sharp serrated knife, slice the end crusts off the pound cake, and level top if it is rounded. Cut the cake horizontally into ½ to ¾ inch slabs (have at least 3 slabs).

2. Rub ricotta cheese through a coarse sieve or strainer into a bowl, using the back of a wooden spoon. Beat cheese with a beater until it is smooth. While beating constantly, add the cream, sugar and liqueur. Fold in chopped fruit and chocolate.

3. Place bottom slab of cake in the center of a serving plate, spread generously with the cheese mixture. Place next slab on top of cheese mixture, lining up sides. Spread with cheese mixture. Repeat, if necessary, ending with a plain slice of cake on the top. Press loaf together lightly, chilling will help stabilize. Refrigerate for at least 2 hours until firm.

4. For Frosting, melt chocolate with coffee in a small heavy saucepan, or in the microwave at a low setting. Stir until chocolate is completely melted. Beat in the chilled butter one piece at a time. Continue beating until chocolate is smooth. Chill frosting until it thickens to spreading consistency. Spread on top, sides and ends of cake.

5. Wrap loosely with plastic wrap and refrigerate for at least 24 hours to ripen. Yield: 8 servings.

1. In a blender or food processor, mix butter, flour and ice water. Press mixture into a 9 inch pie plate. Chill in freezer for 1 hour. Remove from freezer, prick bottom with fork and bake in 425 degree oven for 10 minutes, or until golden.

2. Prepare pudding mix according to package directions. You may substitute cream or half-and-half for the milk if a richer pudding is desired. Pour into cool pie crust.

3. When pudding is set, top with the fruit of your choice.

4. Boil apricot jam and drizzle over tart through a sieve. Chill 1 hour and serve. Yield: 8 servings.

½ **cup butter**
1 **cup flour**
2 **tablespoons ice water**
1 **(3½ ounce) package French vanilla instant pudding**
fresh fruit (grapes, kiwi, strawberries, etc.)
1 **cup apricot jam**

Almond Puff

1 **cup butter or margarine, divided**
2 **cups flour, divided**
1 **cup, plus 2 tablespoons water, divided**
1 **teaspoon almond extract**
3 **eggs**

Powdered Sugar Glaze:

1½ **cups powdered sugar**
2 **tablespoons butter, softened**
1-1½ **teaspoons vanilla extract**
1-2 **tablespoons warm water**
   chopped walnuts or roasted almonds for garnish

1. Heat oven to 350 degrees. Cut ½ cup butter into 1 cup flour. Sprinkle 2 tablespoons water over mixture; mix with a fork. Round into ball, and divide in half. On ungreased baking sheet, pat each half into a 3x12 inch strip, keeping the strips 3 inches apart.

2. In a medium saucepan, heat ½ cup butter and 1 cup water to a rolling boil. Remove from heat and quickly stir in almond extract and 1 cup flour. Stir vigorously over low heat until mixture forms a ball, about 1 minute. Remove from heat. Beat in eggs, all at once, until smooth. Divide in half; spread each half evenly over strips, covering edges completely. Bake about 60 minutes or until topping is crisp and browned. Cool.

3. Mix Glaze ingredients until smooth. Frost strips. Sprinkle with chopped walnuts or chopped roasted almonds. Yield: 8 to 10 servings.

Slice in half lengthwise. Fill with sliced strawberries or fresh sliced peaches, slightly sweetened. Cover with other half. Top with whipping cream and garnish with a piece of fruit from filling.

Next Best Thing to Robert Redford

1. Mix flour, softened butter and pecans together until finely crumbled. Press into a 9x13 inch greased glass baking dish. Bake in 350 degree oven for 15 to 20 minutes. Cool.

2. Beat cream cheese and sugar until smooth. Fold in ½ of the whipped topping and spread over cooled crust. Mix puddings together. Beat with milk until smooth and thick. Spread over middle layer. Top with remaining whipped topping. Grate chocolate for top garnish. Refrigerate overnight. Yield: 12 to 15 servings.

1 cup unsifted flour
½ cup butter or margarine, softened
1 cup finely chopped pecans
1 (8 ounce) package cream cheese
1 cup sugar
1 (12 ounce) carton frozen whipped nondairy topping, divided
1 (6¾ ounce) package instant chocolate pudding
1 (5⅝ ounce) package instant vanilla pudding
3 cups cold milk
grated chocolate for garnish

PRIZE WINNER • CHERRY FESTIVAL

Black Cherry Rum Sauce

1. Mix cornstarch, sugar and water and cook until thick and clear. Add flavoring, coloring and cherries, and cook for 1 minute more.

1 cup water
½ cup sugar
1 tablespoon cornstarch
1 teaspoon lemon juice
1 teaspoon rum extract
1 cup fresh black cherries, halved and pitted
few drops red food coloring

Dry Creek Zinfandel Sorbet

3 cups water
1 cup sugar
3 cups Zinfandel (one 750 ml bottle)
1½ boxes frozen raspberries

1. Put first three ingredients into saucepan. Bring to boil and simmer for 30 minutes to reduce. Remove from heat and add raspberries. Remove mixture to a bowl and refrigerate overnight to macerate flavors.

2. With a sieve, strain out raspberries, put into food processor and puree. Put puree through strainer to remove seeds. Using a wooden spoon to push, work the pulp through a strainer. Add pulp back to Zinfandel juice mixture. Put into ice cream maker and prepare as ice cream, with rock salt and water.

David Stare
Dry Creek Vineyard

Scrumptious Strawberry Dip

4 tablespoons sour cream
1 cup whipped cream or nondairy whipped topping
2 tablespoons brown sugar
1 tablespoon Grand Marnier liqueur
2 tablespoons orange Curaçao liqueur
½ tablespoon rum

1. Stir ingredients together in a small bowl in order listed. Spoon into decorative serving dish or bowl and surround with fresh whole cold strawberries. Yield: 8 servings.

COMMON BAKING PANS & MOLDS		SUBSTITUTIONS	
APPROX. VOLUME	PAN OR MOLD SIZE	IF RECIPE CALLS FOR:	YOU MAY USE:
4 cups	8x4x2½ inch loaf pan	**Baking powder** 1 teaspoon	¼ teaspoon baking soda plus ½ teaspoon cream of tartar
6 cups	8½x4½x2½ inch loaf pan		
8 cups	9x5x3 inch loaf pan		
10 cups	9½x2½ inch spring-form pan	**Cornstarch** 1 tablespoon	2 tablespoons flour
12 cups	10x2½ inch spring-form pan		
6 cups	8x8x1½ inch square pan	**Flour** 1 tablespoon	½ to ⅔ tablespoon cornstarch (for thickening)
8 cups	11x7x1½ inch rectangular pan		
8 cups	8x8x2 inch square pan		
8 cups	9x9x1½ inch square pan		
10 cups	9x9x2 inch square pan	**Flour** 1 cup	1 cup plus 2 tablespoons sifted cake flour
15 cups	13x9x2 inch rectangular pan		
9 cups	9x3½ inch Bundt pan		
12 cups	10x3¾ inch Bundt pan	**Flour** 1 cup	1 cup minus 2 tablespoons sifted all-purpose flour
3 cups	8x1¼ inch pie plate		
4 cups	9x1½ inch pie plate		
4 cups	8x1½ inch cake pan		
6 cups	9x1½ inch cake pan	**Lemon juice** 1 teaspoon	½ teaspoon vinegar
6 cups	9x2 inch pie plate (deep dish)		
7 cups	8x2 inch cake pan	**Milk** 1 cup	½ cup evaporated milk plus ½ cup water
8½ cups	9x2 inch cake pan		
10¾ cups	10x2 inch cake pan		
12 cups	9x3½ inch angel cake pan		
18 cups	10x4 inch angel cake pan	**Sour Milk** 1 cup	1 cup sweet milk plus 1 tablespoon lemon juice or vinegar
4½ cups	8½x2¼ inch ring mold		
8 cups	9¼x2¾ inch ring mold		
6 cups	7x5½x4 inch melon mold	**Sugar** 1 cup	1⅓ cups brown sugar or 1½ cups confectioners' sugar
7½ cups	6x4¼ inch Charlotte mold		

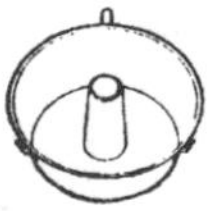

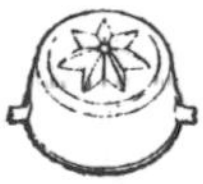

APPROXIMATE EQUIVALENTS

Beans
16 ounces dry — 6-7 cups cooked

Butter or margarine
¼ pound stick — ½ cup

Cheese
4 ounces shredded — 1 cup
8 ounces (cottage) — 1 cup
8 ounces (cream) — 1 cup

Chocolate
1 square — 1 ounce
6 ounces (morsels) — 1 cup

Coconut
3 ounces shredded — 1 cup

Cranberries
12 ounces fresh — 3 cups

Cream
1 cup unwhipped — 2 cups whipped

Cream (sour)
8 ounces — 1 cup

Crumbs (fine, dry)
3 slices bread — 1 cup
28 saltines — 1 cup
22 vanilla wafers — 1 cup
14-15 graham crackers — 1 cup

Egg
1 cup whites — 8-10 eggs
1 cup yolks — 12-14 eggs

Flour
1 pound — 4 cups (sifted)
1 pound — 3½ cups (unsifted)
1 pound (cake) — 4½-5 cups

Garlic (powdered)
⅛ teaspoon — 1 clove

APPROXIMATE EQUIVALENTS

Herbs
1 tablespoon fresh — 1 teaspoon dry

Lemon juice
3 tablespoons — 1 medium lemon

Lime juice
1-2 tablespoons — 1 medium lime

Macaroni
1 cup dry — 2 cups cooked

Meat
1 pound chopped — 3 cups cooked
1 pound ground — 2 cups cooked

Mushrooms
8 ounces fresh — 4 ounces canned

Noodles
1 cup — 1¾ cups cooked

Nuts
4 ounces — 1 cup chopped

Onion
¼ cup fresh — 1 tablespoon dried

Orange juice
⅓-½ cup — 1 medium orange

Raisins
16 ounces — 2½-3 cups

Rice
1 pound — 2 cups
1 cup — 3 cups cooked

Spaghetti
1 pound — 8 cups cooked

Sugar
1 pound granulated — 2 cups
1 pound packed brown — 2¼ cups
1 pound confectioners' — 4-4½ cups

MEASURE	EQUIVALENT
1 teaspoon	⅓ tablespoon (60 drops)
1 tablespoon	3 teaspoons (½ fluid ounce)
2 tablespoons	⅛ cup (1 fluid ounce)
3 tablespoons	1 jigger (1½ fluid ounces)
¼ cup	4 tablespoons (2 fluid ounces)
⅓ cup	5 tablespoons plus 1 teaspoon
⅜ cup	¼ cup plus 2 tablespoons
½ cup	8 tablespoons (4 fluid ounces)
⅝ cup	½ cup plus 2 tablespoons
¾ cup	12 tablespoons (6 fluid ounces)
⅞ cup	¾ cup plus 2 tablespoons
1 cup	16 tablespoons or ½ pint (8 fluid ounces)
1 pint	2 cups (16 fluid ounces)
1 quart	4 cups or 2 pints (32 fluid ounces)
1 gallon	4 quarts or 8 pints or 16 cups (128 fluid ounces)

Children's Home Society of California wishes to thank those who contributed recipes to *Celebrating California*. We regret that we were unable to include many recipes which were submitted due to similarity or availability of space.

Celebrating California Recipe Contributors

Joyce Aftahi
Joann Alton
Millie Ancelet
Anita Anderson
Sue Bartow
Walter Becker
Sara Beeby
Elaine Bender
Marilyn Benson
Edna Bernstein
Valerie Bilham-Boult
Barbara Bonesteel
Kathleen Boulanger
Rosanne M. Boyle
Mary Alice Brady
Gladys Breese
Carmella Breslauer
Sue Bubnack
Lisa Bucher
Pamela Buie
Rose Burtchby
Sally Cambra
Carol Canavero
Joyce Carlisle
Harriette Carr
Carol Carter
Marge Caton
Kim Chambers
Linda Charman
Pat Christie
Phyllis Ciardo
Marian Claassen
Nancy Clark
Pat Cleaver
Jill Colombana
Diane Colyear

Joyce Copeland
Jane Cosgrove
Maria Cramer
Jan Crockett
Clay Curry
Fran Curtis
Sharon Cutri
Lorraine Darienzo
Dave Davis
Denise DeBeneditto
Debbie Del Toro
Mitzi Demman
Jan Dittamore
Carole Dolby
Betty Dowling
Alberta F. Dunbar
Vivian Ebert
Marion Ehlers
Ruth B. Ekberg
Stacy Ekberg
Joel Esperanza
Nancy Espinoza
Melody Favish
Janet Feutz
Jean Fitzwater
Francine Fomon
Chris Foster
Heather Gallagher
Janis Garity
Joani Gist
Peter Goetz
Maureen Goldsmith
Madalynn Gordon
Frances Graham
Dede Grant
Pam Hagstrom

Wolfgang Hanau
Arlyss Hanosh
Lillian Heintz
Gwyn Hicks
Martha Hodge
Candi Hughes
Peggy O'Neil Hyde
Kathleen Hynes
Sunny Johnson
Betsy Jones
Inge Jones
Peggy Jones
Susan Kelley
Richard N. Kelly
Noel Kelsch
Laura Kent
Louise Khasigian
Donna Kilby
Terry Sue Killian
Lynn Kimball
Susan Knoll
Dale Kochenburg
Norma Krawczyk
Dicky Krenz
Niki LaMont
Deno Landa
MaryLou Larrabee
Sharon Larson
Jannis Lauda
Jenoise Leche
Dolores Lindstrom
Tomas Lucia
J. O. Manis
Jane D. Marsh
Pat A. Martin
Sandra Massen

Lidia McCollister
Irene McCormic
Jeannine McDonald
Bruce McDougal
Nancy McDougal
Marjorie McLachlan
Patricia J. Mier
Jeanie Mills
Henriequetta Miralrio
Theresa Mortara
Betty Mroz
Diane Murdoch
Patricia A. Murphy
Rosemary Nachtigall
Marilyn Nash
Christine Nava
Dee Nedom
Betty Newman
Buck Nibler
Richard Nollevaux
Judy Oliphant
Shirley Olsen
Barbara Olwin
Doris Orr
Chris Oswald
Elaine Parkhurst
Andrea Paz
Ruth Paz
Laurie Peters

Gerald D. Petery
Alison Petty
Pat Pfann
Peggy Phister
Anita Poppe
Susan Presar
Steve Pynes
Linda Quinlan
Juaneva Ramirez
Rory Ramirez
Patricia Richards
Alison Riggs
Mary Rodriguez
Jon Rogers
Mary Rogondino
Carole Romero
Debbie Rotert
Marvelle Rottiers
Joann Roubinek
Elaine Salcedo
Maria Sandoval
Nancy Sanford
Lola Scavo
Helga Schulman
Sue Schwaber
Anita See
Debbie Sheesley
Karen Shuman
Linda L. Simpson

Flora Sisson
Claire Smith
Shirley Soderquist
Carolyn Staff
David Stare
M. Starr
Neva Stevenson
Jeanne Steves
Betty Stine
Nancy Stockton
Teddy Strieter
Dick Sutherland
Evie Sutherland
Iva Swift
Penny Tashnick
Velma Thompson
Rosalind Tilson
Tulie Trejo
Sharon Tribowski
Cleta Triplett
Brad Wallace
Hazel Ward
Suzanne Ward
Sybil Ward
Barrie Wentzell
Loreen Wilhelmy
Alice Williams
Barbara Witt

Acknowledgements

Bell-Carter Foods, Inc.   Pearl Richman-Kaiser   Philip and Lillian Heintz

Children's Home Society of California wishes to thank the following auxiliaries for their support of this cookbook project.

Casa de Cuna Auxiliary
Coronado Chapter
La Posada de los Niños
    Auxiliary
Las Amigas del Norte
    Auxiliary
Las Ayudas de los Niños
    Affiliate
Las Companeras
    Ausiliary
Las Duenas Auxiliary
Las Hermanas Auxiliary
Las Munecas Auxiliary
Las Proveedoras del
    Norte Auxiliary
Los Amados Auxiliary
Makua Auxiliary
Niños de la Costa
    Auxiliary
Niños Preciosos
    Auxiliary

Alegro de Niños Auxiliary
Ayundantes Auxiliary
De Acuerdo Auxiliary
Fullerton Auxiliary
Las Brizas del Mar
    Auxiliary
Las Damas del Mar
    Auxiliary
Les Petites Fleurs
    Auxiliary
Newport Harbor Auxiliary
Nightingales Auxiliary
Paso Primero Auxiliary
Santa Ana Auxiliary
Foothill Auxiliary
Leilani Auxiliary
Lullaby Guild Auxiliary of
    CHS
Whittier Auxiliary

Ventura Affiliate

Leprechaun Auxiliary
Los Altos Hills Auxiliary
Sandpiper Auxiliary

Carlmont Auxiliary
Crystal Springs Auxiliary
Ivanhoe Auxiliary
Menlo-Atherton Auxiliary
Rainbow Auxiliary
San Mateo Auxiliary
Starbright Auxiliary
Woodside Auxiliary

ABC Auxiliary
Charlie Brown Auxiliary
Chicken Little Auxiliary
Cinderella Auxiliary
Dumbo Auxiliary
Evergreen Auxiliary
Golden Acorn Auxiliary
Hansel & Gretel Auxiliary
Henny Penny Auxiliary
Highland Jr's Auxiliary
Humpty Dumpty Auxiliary
Kim Auxiliary
Kinderland Auxiliary
Live Oak Auxiliary
Marin Auxiliary
Pandora Auxiliary
Pied Piper Auxiliary
Pixie Auxiliary
Raggedy Ann Auxiliary
Redwood Empire
    Auxiliary
Robin Hood Auxiliary
Rocking Horse Auxiliary
Rose Red Auxiliary
Sleepy Hollow Auxiliary
Thumbelina Auxiliary

Candy Mountain
    Auxiliary
Chipmunk Auxiliary
Fledgling Auxiliary
Golden Goose Auxiliary
Lambkin Auxiliary
Little Papoose Auxiliary
Moppet Auxiliary
River Twins Auxiliary
Rock-A-Bye Auxiliary
Sandman Auxiliary
Sugar Plum Auxiliary
Twinkle Star Auxiliary

Ariels Auxiliary
Auburn Auxiliary
Camellia Auxiliary
Caravan Affiliate
Cotton Heirs Auxiliary
Daisy Auxiliary
Davis Auxiliary
Delta Valley Auxiliary
Dolphins Auxiliary
Enchanted Forest
    Auxiliary
Les Petits Amis Auxiliary
Little Skipper Auxiliary
Littlest Angels Auxiliary
Merry-Go-Round
    Auxiliary
Robinettes Auxiliary
Rosebuds Auxiliary
Silver Spoons Auxiliary
Sonora Auxiliary
Tiny Tim Auxiliary
Treasure Chest Auxiliary
Wishing Well Auxiliary

Celebrating California

FESTIVAL RECIPE INDEX

INDEX

Cookbook il like

-Better Homes and Gardens-
new Bakery book.
1998 meredith Corp.,
Des Moines, Iowa

Ken Haedrich "Country Breakfast"
also see "Home for The Holidays"

CELEBRATING CALIFORNIA

Children's Home Society of California, 7695 Cardinal Ct.
San Diego, CA 92123-3399

Please send ___ copies of **CELEBRATING CALIFORNIA** $17.95 each _____
California residents add sales tax   each _____
Postage and handling   3.00 each _____
                                        Total enclosed $ _____

Name _____

Address _____

City _____ State _____ Zip _____

____ Check or money order enclosed

____ Visa/Mastercard No. _____ Exp. Date _____

Signature _____

Make checks payable to *Children's Home Society Cookbook*.
Profits received by Children's Home Society
will directly benefit children in need in California.

--- --- --- --- --- --- --- --- --- --- --- --- ---

CELEBRATING CALIFORNIA

Children's Home Society of California, 7695 Cardinal Ct.
San Diego, CA 92123-3399

Please send ___ copies of **CELEBRATING CALIFORNIA** $17.95 each _____
California residents add sales tax   each _____
Postage and handling   3.00 each _____
                                        Total enclosed $ _____

Name _____

Address _____

City _____ State _____ Zip _____

____ Check or money order enclosed

____ Visa/Mastercard No. _____ Exp. Date _____

Signature _____

Make checks payable to *Children's Home Society Cookbook*.
Profits received by Children's Home Society
will directly benefit children in need in California.